My Childhood:

Getting Over It

*Healing into the Person You Were
Intended to Be*

By: Elizabeth Papp-Stinson

Praise for:
My Childhood: Getting Over it

Elizabeth leads us through her childhood with an account that is honest, clear and totally disarming. The power of her story is made even more dramatic and profound because she tells her story without judgment or adult commentary. She describes the events with authenticity and excitement of a child, I found myself completely involved with her story. Her poetry is a window into her inner healing self. Her commentary at the end of each chapter, she shares aspects of her journey to become the person she was intended to be. This three-tier approach presents a simple path through traumas, pain and judgments, that, I believe, will open the door for others to encounter and grow from their own wounded childhood."

----- Graham W. Bailey

My Childhood: Getting Over it

REVIEWS FOR THIS 1ST ADDITION

Elizabeth has written an amazing account of healing and "getting over" the pain, abandonment and wounding from her childhood. Those who have worked on their own inner child and family of origin imprints will connect deeply with these writings and those who are just discovering the patterns that come from the early years will open to a whole new world of opportunities for healing and personal growth. Elizabeth will guide readers through her collection of childhood stories, what she learned, how she healed and ends with questions for the reader to contemplate. Thank you to this brave and beautiful soul, Elizabeth, for putting this work together, modeling, being and living the authentic Self.   - Wendyne Limber

"To my forever friend, as I read your story it made me reflect on my own childhood. We all have a story (Happy or Sad). God gives us the ability to pray through, think through and gives us options in all situations. Your story will help us all to cope and deal with our situation to come out healing.   Remember the Bible says: I Chronicle 28:20 "Be strong and courageous, and act; do not fear nor be dismayed, for the Lord God, my God, is with you. He will not fail you nor forsake you until all the work for the service of the house of the Lord is finished."   -- Ethel King

Your story is powerful. I hope many, many people get a chance to read it. No matter what a person's life experiences, there is so much in this story that can help heal the soul." - Al Ritz

"An eye-opener for the reader, harboring incidents, actions, or circumstances from childhood that surface during adulthood. Elizabeth confronts memories stores in her conscious/subconscious clinging to her for years. Very inspiring as she reflects on the story at the end of each chapter. She challenges the reader to release those childhood memories that keep one from healing and being the best, she/he can be. This truly is a journey of survival and moving forward." - Christine Y. Weathers

"I'll never forget the note you wrote to me in your sympathy card after my mother passed away. I still have it. It hit home, as if you somehow knew exactly what I was feeling at that moment. After reading this manuscript I understand it is your gift... A wonderful gift.... To reach out to others through your writing and the person you are. Thank you for sharing it with me." - Debbie Ritz

"The writer, Elizabeth Papp-Stinson, gives a very vivid and descriptive insight or her memories. One would think the hardship of growing up was painful, but the love and laughter were evident in her life experience. Each chapter brings something new... so you must keep reading. You become captive and can almost feel her abuse, pain, suffering and joy she experienced from childhood to adulthood. The book is very well titled, My Childhood: Getting Over it – Healing. Writing this book was HER THERAPY." - Harriet Brown

"I see Elizabeth's soul shining brightly as I read her life's journey. The courage it takes in sharing this beautiful expression of her life. How Elizabeth uses her wonderful teaching and healing abilities to guide you on you healing journey, what a gift Elizabeth is to me and the world. I am honored to call her my friend and colleague. Shine on Elizabeth" – Heartsong

Copyright 2020 by Elizabeth Papp-Stinson

All rights reserved. No part of this publication may be reproduced, scanned, uploaded, stored in a retrieval system, or transmitted, in any form or by any means, electronic, mechanical, photocopying, recording, or otherwise, without the prior written permission of the publisher.

The information and advice contained in this book are based upon the research and the personal and professional experiences of the author. They are not intended as a substitute for consulting with a healthcare professional. The publisher and author are not responsible for any adverse effects or consequences resulting from the use of any of the suggestions, preparations, or procedures discussed in this book. All matters pertaining to your physical health should be supervised by a healthcare professional. It is a sign of wisdom, not cowardice to seek a second or third opinion.

Childhood: Getting Over it / Elizabeth Papp-Stinson.

214 pages cm

Cover Design by Elizabeth Papp-Stinson

Design by Elisabeth Papp-Stinson

ISBN: 978-1-736-1520-1-0 (pp)

ISBN: 978-1-7361520-2-7 (ebook)

1st edition, April 2021

Printed in the United States of America

10 9 8 7 6 5 4 3 2 1

Dedicated to:

Joann Marie (Agle) Conrad

1949-2017

For laughing and crying with me when I originally shared my childhood stories with you. For starting every conversation, phone or otherwise, with the question, "So, how's the book coming?" or "Have you started your book yet?" Your encouragement and belief in me planted a seed that didn't grow during your season on the planet and since your passing was watered, fed, and finally sprouted and grew into this book. Thank you, my dear, I have talked to you daily while writing my stories, and I am still hearing your voice in my head; I miss you.

Acknowledgments

Thank you, my husband Ron, for your patience and ability to let me cry when I needed without interrupting my process. Your love to watch, listen, and not react. Thank you for listening to my stories as I read them out loud. Never judging the story or my reaction to it, for letting me vent without needing to fix it. You always help me up when I fall, and support me until I can walk on my own. I love and appreciate you more than you know, my partner in life.

I want to acknowledge my brothers and sisters for how they shaped my childhood, with shared love, fear, and growth. We moved through childhood together and still experienced our traumas and perceptions individually developing distinct patterns we would carry on throughout our adulthood. I would not be who I am today without each of you and the many contributions, admonishments, humor, and love we shared. Love, love each one of you with all my heart can generate.

Thank you, Wendyne Limber and the Soulville community for being there for every moment of my therapy. For allowing me to express my tears, anger, and insecurities without judging. Loving and supporting, no matter how loud I screamed, swore, and released my trauma. Each of you sharing yourself with me and letting me share myself with the group. You all taught me about connectedness with humanity, each of us sharing our journey and all of its ugliness and beauty. Thank you Wendyne, for witnessing my growth and leading me to the next level with support, patience, and mostly your loving spirit. You pushed me at exactly the right time and were honest in the kindest way. Your Support and always guiding me to the next phase of healing. Love you Wendyne, to the Fifth Dimension and back.

My Childhood: Getting Over it

Petrina McGowen, my therapist, and writing mentor, and instructor loving me through all of my process. Letting me express, vent, explore, and mostly cry and release without "shoulding." Encouraging me to write what I needed to in your writing class, always nudging no matter how bad I thought my writing was. Teaching and showing me what and how to express love for myself. Petee, you were a random phone call to a therapist that changed my life. A journey into the highest exploration of myself. You gave me the encouragement, support, and suggestions that morphed into this book. I love you and the love you exude to everyone around you. Always bringing me back to love.

My children, Andrew, Christopher, Renee, and Melanie, who never discouraged me from pursuing my therapies. You listened with patience as I sorted through my childhood. Thank you for not judging my process and not saying, "Mom, why are you doing this to yourself?" For not judging my moods, odd behaviors, and at times my isolation. I am joyous when I say I am proud of each of you and your gentlest of spirits. I love you guys with all I have.

My little sister Esther, thank you for listening to my feelings and emotions without interjecting your own stories or versions of them. You let me vent and express myself about these childhood stories. Never making light of them or comparing them to your own. Your generosity in listening with love allowed me to own my stories without diluting them. My connectedness to your soul grows daily with the love we share.

Acknowledgments

Terri Foley, my neighbor, movie buddy, and gracious friend, thank you for being the first person to read my completed manuscript. Your feedback reassured me to keep pursuing my dream of publishing this book. Your first review helped me get over my writer's quicksand thinking that it's not good enough and no one wants to hear these "my" stories. Your enthusiasm and encouragement moved me forward. Love you.

Carolyn Kott Washburne, my patient editor who was honest and encouraging in all her comments, edits, and suggestions. You gave me the confidence after each group of edits to open myself up even more in telling and showing with words. Thank you for responding quickly to my thoughts and words and keeping this book moving forward. How I found you through a friend of a friend of a friend was not a coincidence and was meant to be. Thank you.

Contents

Dedicated to: .... *i*
Acknowledgments. .... *iii*
Introduction. .... *xi*
How to Get the Most from this Book. .... *xiii*

The backstory/history: 1
Three to Six Months Old An Early Imprint 15
Age Four; Asleep on the Couch 17
Age Five; Please God. 21
Age Five; Saturday Girls' Night 25
Age Five; Running. 29
Age Seven; Grandpa Papp's Visit 33
Age Seven; My Guitar 39
Age Eight; Lice Treatment 43
Age Eight; The Swimming Pool 47
Age Eight; The Missing Toe 51
Age Eight; Nicks with Dad 55
Age Eight; Green House on Texas Street 59
Age Eight; Pee Pie Revenge 63
Age Nine; The Dairy. 67
Age Nine; Mom Quits Smoking. 73
Age Nine; Chiller. 77
Age Ten; Popping Canning Jars 81
Age Ten; Church Candy Fundraising 85
Age Eleven; Fifty-Cent Food Coupons 91
Age Eleven; Tooth Extraction 95
Age Eleven; Church Tent Revival. 99

Age Eleven; Messin' Kids 105
Age Eleven; Children DisciplingChildren 109
Age Twelve; Desegregation by Busing 113
Age Twelve; Getting Evicted 117
Age Twelve; The R-Wing 121
Age Twelve; Shoe Shining. 127
Age Twelve; Children Shoplifting. 131
Age Twelve; Mom Walking Out. 135
Age Twelve; Getting Mugged 139
Age Thirteen; Haunted House 143
Age Thirteen; White Tablecloths. 147
Age Thirteen; Tea with No Sugar 151
Age Fourteen; Free Samples 155
Age Fourteen; Apu Getting Off the Bus 159
Age Fourteen; Encyclopedias 165
Age Sixteen; Dislocating My Elbow 169
Age Sixteen; Where Are You, God? 173
Age Sixteen; Change in Dad's Pocket. 179
Age Sixteen; My First Sexual Experience 183
Age Sixteen; Miscarriage 187
Age Eighteen; An Adult. 191
EPILOGUE. 195

Introduction

I write this book out of love, love for myself, my family, my readers. To share my stories and history and how it shaped my tender young life. Confronting my past allows me to live in my future and in all the present moments in between.

I immersed myself in transpersonal psychotherapy. I grappled with my history, overwhelmed with feelings, shame, anger, and self-loathing. This therapy moved me to work through my childhood and past wounding's giving me awarenesses, letting me become aware, release, and replace my patterns and beliefs from my trauma. With the help of several therapists and my tribe of wonderfully compassionate people at Soulville, a sacred healing took place. This therapy allowed me to release trauma from my body and soul. I used methods of screaming, sobbing, punching pillows, writing, dancing, singing, breathwork, meditation, yoga, myofascial release, acupuncture and more. I wanted to, no, needed to express myself and the childhood I experienced to record it and set it free.

My secondary reason for writing this book is to let you read my stories and know that there is a place of understanding, healing, and thriving after trauma. Yes, it's work, yes, it's hard, and there will be tears and feelings, and on the other side you will step into your true self. All of us long to be who we are and to fulfill our destiny here on the earth. My hope for every reader is to find the courage to begin their own journey into self-fulfillment and authenticity. I hope the short story versions connect you to your own experiences and trigger feelings toward your own stories and activates the parts of your unconscious that long for healing.

Last, I'd want readers to acknowledge children, their needs, abuses, longings, and how security and personality are affected by trauma. How does a child behold the world controlled by adults, how do they learn rules, love, acceptance, and self-importance in the world they are growing up in? Kids are aware of the world around them and yet are not aware of all they absorb. They grow up identifying who they are consciously and subconsciously, unaware of how much the unconscious controls their lives as they grow up to and through adulthood.

As I grew into adulthood, I became what I experienced in childhood abandonment, not belonging, fear, anger, and so many feelings I had to shut down to survive to adulthood. I reached adulthood with patterns of disassociating with reality ingrained in my way of being. Living under the delusion of having control over my life and decisions. To unravel myself, I had to go back to my childhood and recognize where I came from, who I was and how I was raised.

My parents lacked the capacity to raise a healthy, nurturing family. Throughout their parenting, they compromised their children's emotional health by adding hurdles that children could not conquer. Having ten children, mental illness, alcoholism, physical abuse, religious abuse, poverty, addictions and violence all impacted my adult life. These stories show how their own lacking affected my life and what I have learned.

How to Get the Most from this Book

Today my journey continues, and I know that I am not my stories. I know my history; it has shaped and impacted who I have become today. I love my life, myself, and the humbling love in and around humanity as souls seek to teach and learn from each other and realize their destiny.

Each story has my approximate age at the time of the story. I used the memory of the house I lived in at the time of the story to help in determining my age, for example:

Age Four
Asleep on the Couch

Each story has an original poem that can be read before or after each, or both. These poems are my original poems, and include my pain, expressions and healings.

I tried to keep the last page of each chapter blank for your own reflections, notes and entries you may want to explore.

At the end of each story, in italics, are my notes and they include what I know now. and my answers to three questions:

1. What experiences do I want to take away from my story?

2. How am I going to grow from my childhood story?

3. How can I give back to the world?

The backstory/history:

Dad/Apu

My father grew up in the small town of Demecser, Hungary with five brothers and two sisters. He was an educated young man, with demons of his own from his alcoholic father. My grandfather, when drunk, tortured his family, abused his kids and wife, and, when sober, lived as the iconic angry man. He ruled his domain by beating the rules into anyone daring to disobey or question. My grandmother inhabited a religious soul, graceful, quiet, and full of love and empathy. She was gentle with children, and walked with her head bent downward, never wanting to bring attention to herself for fear of retribution.

My grandfather would lock his sleeping, pajama-clad family out of the house in the dead of winter with neighbors having to shelter them from the cold. He played Russian roulette once with his offspring during a drunken episode. I heard other horrific stories of beatings and hospitalizations until his children were of age to escape his reign. The scars from my father's traumas eventually touched and created new wounds on each of his children.

As my father grew into young adolescence, he ran wild with the boys in his town, drinking, carousing, gambling, and getting into trouble. Before leaving for the army, he met my mother as she walked to school while he was hanging around town. He became infatuated with her and followed her one day as she took a path to the store and raped her. Seeking permission to marry her, he went to her parents,

My Childhood: Getting Over it

and they refused, knowing his reputation and because my mom was only sixteen. Several months later he returned to my grandparents, announcing my mother's pregnancy and how they must consent to the marriage. Mom was sixteen and dad was twenty-two.

Later, as a freedom fighter, he committed and witnessed war atrocities. During a visit to Hungary, my uncle shared with me one incident of my father as a freedom fighter in Hungary. He told me the story as we sat eating gelato at a table outside the building where my father shot a German soldier to death as he begged my dad to spare his life, for his wife and children.

The Hungarian Revolution of 1956 was a spontaneous nationwide revolution against the Hungarian People›s Republic and its Soviet-imposed policies, it lasted from October 23 until 10 November 1956. It was the first major threat to Soviet control since the Red army drove Nazi Germany from its territory at the End of World War II in Europe.

The revolt began when thousands of students protested and marched through central Budapest to the Hungarian Parliament building, using a van with loudspeakers. When they demanded a delegation's release, they were fired upon from within the building. Multiple students died and one was wrapped in a flag and held above the crowd. The revolt spread throughout Hungary and the government collapsed. Thousands organized themselves into militias, battling the ÁVH (State protection authority) and Soviet troops.

On 4 November, a large Soviet force invaded Budapest and other regions of the country. The Hungarian resistance continued until 10 November. During the conflict, 700 soviet troops and over 2,500 Hungarians were killed. 200,000 Hungarians fled as refugees fearing retribution. In Austria, large refugee camps were constructed from

The backstory/history:

which emigration to other countries was arranged for the many refugees who escaped across the border prior to the military closure.

The name Freedom fighters was given to the Hungarian militia that fought the revolution by the free world press.

My dad turned to alcohol just like his dad to relieve and forget his painful traumas. His anger emerged during most of his alcoholic episodes, which he took out on his wife and children. I can describe dad as a womanizer and gambler, always seeking high-stakes thrills and excitement to feel alive. This energy gave him the belief in having the power to rescue and provide for his family with his great, imagined gambling wins. As his addictions grew, he struggled to show love to his family, not wanting to appear weak or too proud to admit failure. He grew up with Old World beliefs and ways of life, escaped to America at twenty-seven, entering a new world culture, language, career, religion, and a child arriving just about every year.

Once in America, Apu (Dad) immediately separated himself from my mother's brother who had escaped with them. Apu stood in line, waiting for a city assignment that needed his trade. Uncle Attila told him to tell the man behind the counter his trade was a tool and die maker, so both their destinations would guarantee Milwaukee, Wisconsin. After hearing that bakers were much needed in Rochester, New York, (the Flour/Flower city) he told the clerk he was a baker even though his hands had never touched flour. Now assigned to New York State, he was free to pursue a fresh start in America with no threats or interference from his brother-in-law.

My Childhood: Getting Over it

Apu got a job and Mom's pregnancy handicapped her in the unfamiliar country, not knowing the language or neighborhood.

They moved around for the first five to six years, renting larger apartments as the family grew.

Men worked and women stayed at home and raised the children who must listen and behave. Dad demanded no crying or talking back, and each one of us had to be studious and smart. His children could not have disabilities, weaknesses, or failures. He worked to provide and enjoy what he provided for his family during leisure times and holidays, playing as hard as his children. He would throw his body on the ground to stop the ball during kickball and he would run and jump with us during volley ball games. His energy and spirit matched ours with ease. We would laugh with him as he boasted about skiing with the Gabor sisters in Hungary, which we knew even as he told us that he was joking. Dad often spoke proudly of the fact that he never drank at home and his children never witnessed him drink. No, we never saw him drinking. We felt the effects of his drinking and analyzed his walk to determine a good, bad, or violent drunk arriving. When violence arrived, it swept through the house, banging into everyone in its path. Screams, terror, blood, bruises, and, finally, police arriving, hopefully to take him away for the night so we had a sense of safety and peace while we slept.

As a kid, I recognized his deep haunting violence as anger. I didn't understand how it came to be, yet I saw it rise and settle periodically, never healing, never leaving him. When my dad would call me "Honey" in his gentlest tone, I understood it meant "I love you" even though he never said the words to me. He gave what he had emotionally, physically, and spiritually. Not necessarily what I thought I needed.

The backstory/history:

I learned life from my father; he showed me what the joy of generosity and hard work looked like. I stared at glimpses of a happy family and love coming through personal anguish and pain. He had a wonderful faculty for humor and was not afraid to appear silly to his children, however, never with adults.

Apu had an infectious joyous energy when he could relax and wasn't struggling. He pointed out personalities to me, describing them in detail. Telling me how a person with a stingy attitude could express itself in my world if I let that person into my life. Never to expect a giving spirit because their pattern of saving is all they know. He would show me people that walked with the weight of the world on their shoulders to witness the physical effects it has on them and showed me how little they enjoyed life. His observations on people that made bad decisions and where they were in life as we watched them. He was unaware that I was also watching him and comparing what he said to his patterns and habits. His personal demons were always close by, and I grasped them as I grew up alongside him. Inserting the knowledge he was imparting on me, and watching, I was always watching him and the world around me, absorbing.

Working tirelessly during his lifetime, he ended up doing heavy manual work as he aged. When alcohol completely took over his life, he couldn't keep a job and took work with whoever would hire him.

In his later years, my Dad became homeless, depleted of worldly possessions and yet trying desperately to maintain the facade of being okay, when showing up to family holiday functions.

I wept silently for him as he smiled and joked with his grand-

My Childhood: Getting Over it

kids and children, knowing he was returning to the streets that night, too proud to accept help and have his children think of him as a failure.

Through this veneer, I could feel and see his shame.

As I got older, I came to terms with his capabilities, and knew I would never receive the parent I wanted and learned to let go of those wishes. Throughout my childhood, Apu was the parent who gave me pause, thought, and introspection into humanity. Why is he doing that? Does he have remorse? Does he love? Where is his love? Will he change? Can he change? How could he be so gentle and foolish and also so violent? I questioned why he had so much anger and hate. I learned to recognize these same traits in others around me, and later in myself.

With a significant work on myself, I realized I received exactly what I needed from him and thanked him for the fullness of the life he gave me. I observed, listened, and took it in. These experiences are stored in my consciousness, subconsciousness, my body and my spirit. Dad, one of my greatest teachers of heart, death, and the sad, painful, joyous, and messy living that happens in between. He gave me a profound understanding of addiction, the pain that defines one's soul, and the value and disregard society puts on someone suffering from addiction. I watched him struggle with several addictions, that slowly stripped away his energy, and spirit, reducing his life to self-imprisonment. He was living for the addictions only, everything around him fell away, no longer important, loyal to the next drink or gambling opportunity.

The backstory/history:

I now know that every soul on the planet deserves to heal from their pain and trauma. I loved my dad as a child does and then slowly watched his essence deteriorate and leave him depleted. This allowed me to love him with an open heart, knowing he suffered in part for me. For my soul to explore my own painful abandonment, fear, and love so deeply and to witness what pain can do to another soul never receiving his own healing.

Yes, his demons awoke during his drunken tirades, and still he had a gentle side, an entertainer of storytelling, and talking politics. He could observe situations and comment so spot on with people's personalities as he made light of them being careful not to put them down personally. He exaggerated their faults to the point of silliness that made me laugh without judgment. Dad would make up stories if Mr. John was visiting from down the street, because he kept looking at his watch and after Mr. John left, dad would say yep, Mr. John didn't want to get hit in the head with the frying pan by Mrs. John, that's why he kept looking at his watch, he didn't want a flat head so he left. He would have a story about the little old lady pulling her cart home from the grocery store, in detail about how her husband died and she never drove so now she has to shop with the cart and tow it home. I would ask him if he knew her and her husband and he would just answer, no, I never met them. One of the parishioners in church would always fall asleep during the church service and on the ride home dad would exaggerate his snoring as being loud enough to scare the sinners to the altar. We would all break out in laughter.

His generosity prevailed even as a detriment to himself. He once invited a homeless couple to live with us for months because the woman was pregnant. He just couldn't let a pregnant woman live on the streets. He worked tirelessly to help them get a place of their own.

My Childhood: Getting Over it

I watched this couple enter our home, smelling terrible, with dirt-caked feet that took my breath away. Her feet were black, hard, and calloused because she never wore shoes. I came to know them and expected the baby's birth. I witnessed the struggle between these lost souls, trying to find their way. My dad's way of being in the world was complex. He encompassed many traits: spontaneity, humor, haunted anger, fear, violence, joy and love.

When Apu passed away, my family met at the nursing facility to view him before they transferred his body to the funeral parlor. One of my thoughts after leaving the facility and turning onto the intersection near my home: I will never turn a corner to unexpectedly see my dad waiting for me. His unforeseen arrivals started with my first job at sixteen. Whenever I exited a building, I would always do a 360 to see if my dad was waiting for me, ready to ask for money. Fear always rose when this happened; I feared the scene he would make if I said no, fear of him asking for too much. I had to process the date quickly to determine my rent due date and what I had already saved toward it so far. I learned later this sense of relief didn't cover the amount of healing I needed to recover from the other fears from my childhood.

Mom

My mother was six years younger than Apu, and she only completed the fifth grade. She married my dad at age sixteen. They escaped Hungary during the reformation in 1956. They escaped to Vienna, Austria, with mom and a group of friends and relatives, leaving my oldest sister behind.

The backstory/history:

Mom refused to continue on to America without her daughter, sending Apu and a few other men back to Hungary to retrieve her.

At twenty, she arrived in the U. S. and at Thirty-four, she gave birth to her eleventh child. She was pregnant, and with a preschooler. Not knowing the language, customs, and neighborhood, she stayed at home. Because of my mother's isolation and language barrier her ability to discuss birth control and manage pregnancies was out of her reach. And so, a baby arrived virtually every year. Mom resolved her pregnancy issue by deciding not to have sex any more after her eleventh child's birth with her intrauterine device (IUD), birth control became imbedded in her uterus during her entire pregnancy. She had tried every birth control available and the IUD was her last resort and it too failed her. Her religious belief did not allow her to have her tubes tied, she believed she would be intervening in God's will.

She relied on and had a deep Pentecostal faith. When in Hungary, she was catholic, and after a short time in America she became a member of the Assembly of God Pentecostal Church. She was so impressed by the minister walking the neighborhood to invite people to his church and also for providing transportation to and from church that she joined this new faith. Speaking and understanding Hungarian at the time, she continued to attend as long as she was able and she understood more as her language improved deepening her faith. She didn't want to understand politics and ignored the sophistication of society while she strived to love and share love. She left her family behind in Hungary to start a new life in America. The soviet military occupation (government) in power at the time killed her dad, who also worked for the government, to set an example for others who thought they could leave the country and their family behind without repercussions.

My Childhood: Getting Over it

Mom carrier the guilt of her dad's execution throughout her life, never putting it down.

She forgave and gave so generously to family and strangers. If you needed something, and she had it, it belonged to you. I can remember her giving away vegetables to her neighbors after returning from the public market. She would prepare a dish for an elderly neighbor after making a feast on Sundays. Mom could always save and had a stash of money available for whoever needed it. She was sensitive to the needs of others and noticed who was disadvantaged around her. I would watch her help another disheveled mother at the grocery store with money, quieting a child, or just saying hello in her gentle way. I watched her on Mother's Day give a neighbor one of the two flats of flowers I had just given her. The neighbor who did not get a visit from her children that Sunday, mom telling the woman that she had more flowers than she could plant.

She had what the doctor diagnosed as a "nervous breakdown" after her eleventh child's birth after Apu lost our family home in a card game. The doctors called it a "nervous breakdown" not knowing that she had just given birth to her eleventh child while facing eviction from her home in a few weeks. My dad told the doctor he just didn't understand why she cried for hours at a time. The prescribed shock treatments changed her, and she lost a lot of her memory. The mother who returned after these treatments was disoriented, sad, unfocused, and unconnected with her children for a long time. She shared with me many times her vision of suffering, and she said, "God showed her at a young age that she should expect much suffering in this lifetime."

And that she did.

The backstory/history:

A genius in all household matters, she always saved no matter how little money flowed in. Her offers of generosity were so genuine that one did not refuse her gift, no matter how small. As we all went to school and learned to read, we would teach mom to read and speak English. She always spoke "broken" English and mixed up words, but you were able to understand her and giggle at some of the words she used and pronounced as she spoke. I could listen to her talk for hours as she described events and people in her beautifully accented English. She cooked the most delicious meals many times with so little. Before her shock treatments, I remember many church parishioners coming over for dinner after the Sunday morning church service. The meal, discussions, and fellowship went on for hours, ending in a delicious dessert.

Mom taught me my sense of kindness and gentleness. She pointed out others' needs for me to contemplate. My sense of empathy came through her understanding and sharing with me how to see others suffering and to search inside myself for my internal empathy for them. She showed me what a deep belief in faith looked like. As I aged, I recognized that faith in humanity existed in each soul on the planet. Human frailties, strengths, and hopes show up in so many arenas and simple moments. She opened the crack that allowed me to begin to understand that religion wasn't what gave you faith, it was the belief in yourself and the power within that gave you the strength and love to move through life's lessons not just for yourself but for others. The love comes from within, not without.

When I was a child, one-on-one time with my mother was almost impossible, yet she found opportunities to give of herself. I remember complaining to her one morning that the tooth fairy had not left any money under my pillow. The washing machine was broken,

My Childhood: Getting Over it

and mom was sorting loads of clothing while I went on about everyone else getting money from the fairy and she forgot about me. My mother continued sorting and then loading baskets of clothes into a red wagon. She got her purse and instructed me to hold on to the top two baskets in the wagon. I got even madder, thinking she hasn't heard a word I said, and now she wanted me to help her. As she towed the wagon down Lyell Avenue, a busy city street full of shops and businesses, she didn't speak until we stopped in front of a diner. The story was that the tooth fairy told my mother to take me out to breakfast instead of giving me a dime for my tooth—my first time out to breakfast, and with just my mother. I sat at the table swinging my little legs, looking out the window at the red wagon piled high with dirty clothes. She found a way to make me feel special, get her work done, and get me to help her with it. I cherish the memory and the wisdom.

    My time with my mother usually entailed some kind of work or cooking. She never used words to tell me how to do it, she would show me and then hand me the spoon, hoe, fruit to peel, or diaper to change. If I did it incorrectly, she showed again and then gave me an affirmative nod if performed correctly. It was during these times that I learned and imbedded the role of the family hero. I understood early that my job would be mommy's helper in all things—the children, cooking, cleaning, and taking over when needed. As a young child, I relished the time with her and felt special until those times arose when I absolutely felt I could not handle the task assigned. I hated to be left in charge of my younger siblings, because there were so many of them and they would overwhelm me. I didn't have the capability to watch them all at the same time and would resort to hitting them to keep them from destroying the house. I would feel like I had betrayed them when this happened and it took away from the bond, we shared of just being brother or sister. Hitting was the only discipline I knew

The backstory/history:

to use to control children. Those were the times that stayed with my unconscious, telling me I wasn't good enough, powerful enough, capable enough. Unconsciously those times lay dormant in my soul. I was not only incapable, I created additional animosity, anger and chaos in future relationships especially with my siblings.

As you will read, I watched my mother's suffering throughout my childhood and as an adult have pondered so many times: How my mother could even stand upright? Her stamina in life was a testament to motherhood, womanhood, and power. I saw her lose everything three times in her life and still continue to move forward. She would always continue to present herself as ready with the hope of something better coming. She loved her children and with a gentle touch to your head, a quick hug, or with just a smile across the room she could make you feel special. Offerings of food were always offerings of love. On visits to her home, she would make me a liverwurst or bologna sandwich. I would tell her, "Mom, I don't eat meat," she would then ask, "Do you want a ham sandwich then?" I would have to remove the meat from the sandwich myself to create a lettuce and tomato sandwich. To which she would shake her head, implying, Why bother? Mom could make me laugh just watching her. She would communicate half in English and half in Hungarian. It would drive my husband crazy. He would turn to me and say, "Well, I got half of it, I think she said, '"she wants to go to the market on Saturday."'

Mom was one of the gentlest, most generous spirits I have encountered in this world. She taught me so much that I am aware of, and I know more will arise from my unconsciousness in the future as memories of her remind me of her spirit.

Three to Six Months Old
An Early Imprint

One of my mother's early shared memories of me as an infant happened at three months when my mother left me in my crib. Apu wanted to go to the annual Hungarian-American Club picnic, and Mom had just put me down to sleep. After much argument, Apu convinced her to leave me while I napped, and he promised they would be back soon. So, they took off, Mom, Apu and my two older sisters, leaving me comfortably asleep. They returned home late in the evening, Apu drunk, my sisters tired and my mother finally coming to my rescue. She described the scene to me when she took me out of the crib. I was inconsolable, wet and soiled, my eyes swollen from salty tears, screaming, with my little body shaking with rage and need.

Why did my mother share this story with me? Was she assuaging her guilt, unknowingly giving me vital trauma information on where my core issue of abandonment originated? Or was she just sharing because she didn't realize the impact it had on my life? She believed that as an infant I didn't remember the incident? I could not comprehend the sheer terror of crying for hours as a baby with no one coming to my rescue. I know this experience stayed in my unconscious and my body and gave me my first impression of life. Abandonment, feeling like death to my tiny self.

My Childhood: Getting Over it

What I have learned from hearing about one of my first experiences in this world is that my body and mind kept this memory through its sensory brain (the limbic system). I did not have the voice or ability to express my feelings of dying. The talking part of my brain, hadn't developed yet. My body held onto this memory and so did the limbic system. My survival instincts being threatened created a pattern of belief in my subconscious before I could express my core belief in being secure and cared for. My infant self, cried out for someone to come, to feed me, to change me for hours and no one came to my aid. My needs were not being addressed, my basic survival rights were impacted and imbedded. I was not comforted (loved) as I cried out for hours with no response. I have cried tears for my infant self and promised to keep her safe and to love her unconditionally. I can speak for her now and let go of the beliefs and patterns that hid in the limbic brain, waiting to be released.

After my mother made me aware of this story, I discovered several core beliefs, that I carried through adulthood, regarding my sense of safety and survival. I worked to change these beliefs because of my awareness of how profound the experience was for my infant self. The healing work on my past beliefs allowed me to change my perspective of how I move through life as an adult. I now know I am safe, loved, worthy of love and no longer need to hold onto those early traumatic events as truths of who I should be. I can give my inner child nurturing as she needs it and whenever she needs it.

My hope is for you, the reader, to look into your birth story, stories of your infancy, before you spoke, and make some connections. Explore your beliefs in life and others and then question them. Question their truth. Release those beliefs and replace them with new, powerful beliefs that will serve you now as an adult with the voice and strength you now have to change. Use your strength to give your inner child the security and love it needs to heal. Hold her in your mind and heart, tell her she is loved and safe

Age Four;
Asleep on the Couch

No matter how young, preverbal even.

A child recognizes, feels, keeps

born into this humanness

the call of the soul's subconscious

the stuff that transforms

1st teaching

Oneness, connection and LOVE

Will I reconcile

Will I heal

In this lifetime?

My Childhood: Getting Over it

I am a young child, not yet in school, asleep on the couch, and awaken to hushed pleadings and complaining. It's dark, and I am oblivious of time. The sobbing gets louder as I stir. The sofa holds many smells that surround me: food, sweat, dust, baby urine, and smelly feet. My thoughts and ears register verbal exchanges. As my eyes open, I try to focus on the sounds. My parents' bed is centered in the middle of the dining room directly across from me, which opens with a large archway. They are using this as their bedroom and are arguing in Hungarian. My mom is pleading with my father to stop; she is having her period. What is he doing? Why is he upsetting my mother? Eyes closed; I lay still so they don't know I am awake. Time passes, the crying stops. I see my mom's shadow walk past me to the bathroom. She returns to bed and everything is quiet again. I cannot know the depth of what just happened. I feel fear, heartache, and the need to save and take care of my mother as it becomes imprinted in my child's subconscious.

The next day I wake, Dad has left for work, everyone is waking up, and Mom is busy in the kitchen. As my thoughts return to the night, the dining room calls to me and I satisfy my child's curiosity. I see blood on the sheets and a knife on the window ledge. Again, I feel anxious because I can't make sense of last night's suffering and what I observe this morning. I grasp that Mom did not choose it to happen, and it hurt her. The person carrying out the abuse was my dad, my champion, the man who makes me laugh and feel good about myself. I know I must look after my mother and now I also know that my dad can hurt her.

Age Four; Asleep on the Couch

It takes years to realize how my role as my mother's protector connected to this event. My mom's and my positions reversed that day, and this reversal was reinforced during my lifetime with many incidents of violence against her by my dad. I learned to call the police and stand between my parents' physical fights. My responsibility developed into caretaker, fighter, financier, and watcher of my mother's well-being. The boundaries vanished between myself and my mother at this young age, and we became enmeshed. I have always felt a deep grief within myself, never knowing I had sacrificed love, self-love, replacing it with responsibility for my mother. That was my new definition of love. I now know that even though I didn't understand what happened, it registered deep within me and changed my role in the family for years to come.

I also know that I can change the role I play with my family. The protector obligation to my parents is not my responsibility. I can give up speaking for my siblings and let them have their own memories and relationship with my parents. Judgment is not mine to have, and forgiveness is completely up to me. No one may force their responsibility on me.

I would encourage you to ask yourself the hard questions about what your responsibility is to not only your parents but to the rest of your family. Do they come first? Why don't you come first? You are born to this planet to fulfill your destiny first. Once you truly love and realize yourself you will know your boundaries, responsibilities and how far you need to go with others. Always put the oxygen mask on yourself first. It is not selfish; it is your responsibility, the reason you are here, for yourself first. It doesn't mean your love is any less for others -- and self-love is the power behind all the love that flows from you. Who are you enmeshed with?

Age Five; Please God

Where are you, my highest power?

Are you listening . . . ?

can you acknowledge me?

hear my little soul's sobs and pleadings

feel the confusion, desperation, and need

Hear me, please,

Release me from this pact

I don't think I can handle it

I am but a child; I don't understand.

Please, God

My Childhood: Getting Over it

It is late at night; I have been asleep for a while. I wake to loud screams and yelling. Mom and Dad are fighting again. As I get out of my bed, I peek down to the end of the hall; I see a light illuminating my parents at the top of the stairs. The stairway has thick spindles that you can see through to the lower level. I walk to investigate. My mother is very pregnant and hanging onto the banister, while my father is trying to push her down the steps.

My oldest sisters' bedroom is right next to the staircase. The screaming continues, and Mom is begging for my sister to help. Big sis comes out of her room to yell at my dad. I look at Apu, and he yells at me to go to bed. I run to bed and hide under the covers, shaking uncontrollably. Crying and praying, I ask the Lord to please make him quit drinking. I can tell he is drunk; I beg God and to seal the deal I promise to behave and never sin again. My mother yells out that he has the baby's head. I cannot picture what she means; She keeps repeating he's hurting the baby's head. I try to envision the baby in my mother's belly and how my dad can hurt his skull.

I'm shaking again, a reaction I get during these traumatic episodes. It is hard to control this shaking. I run out to the stairwell again thinking about the babies head scream as loud as I can at my father, telling him to stop hurting my mother and the baby. Dad suddenly stops and heads downstairs. My sister returns to her room and Mom sobs quietly as she crawls into bed with her. The light in the hall is bright. I do not turn it off and return to bed listening . . . to see if Apu comes upstairs again. I am on high alert and still somehow fall asleep.

Age Five; Please God

My child's psyche does not have the vocabulary to interpret or handle this traumatic incident, and again I hold it in my mind and body. I wait for a release, knowing my small voice has so much screaming to be heard. It became a habit for me to not share my sadness, which grows into a deep, trapped heartache. A grief that has some release, only when the pressure inside explodes outward because it could no longer remain contained. When liberty arrives, it again causes uncontrollable trembling. My body returning to the original trauma—letting go. I have learned to allow this shaking and release now and honor it when it happens. Sometimes it's just a shudder, when I see or hear anger expressed by someone and it resonates through my body. Other times, when my pain rises, I let myself feel deeply and release to heal.

I grow from these experiences as I recognize them, knowing that I am healing each time I become conscious of the history of the feeling. The birth of the trauma and then the connection to how it has shaped my thoughts and feeling process to today. This awareness is such an enormous part of the shift that arrives with the healing.

When your feelings arise, look deeper to where they originate and sit with it and what it represents. Is it abandonment, anger for the shame you are holding, rage for not being heard or dismissed? Ask yourself, where does this belief come from and is it still true today? Become conscious of what your feelings represent— you possess the power to change and heal that belief with your adult experiences and wisdom. You don't have to carry your childhood beliefs anymore if you don't want to.

Age Five; Saturday Girls' Night

Belonging

Acceptance as a member

A basic human hunger

A place recognized without language

A feeling, a craving, to be a part . . .

primal to our sense of being

to know happiness

Maslow charts it as

the third psychological need

connection, love

Belonging

My Childhood: Getting Over it

I will start kindergarten soon, and I realize that an unknown world is opening up around me. It's Saturday night and Mom is in the living room braiding my sisters' hair and putting her own hair in rollers. This is the Saturday evening routine I've never been privy to: preparing for Sunday and church. Usually Mom makes time to put bobby pins in my hair to make it curly and sends me to bed with the other small children. Tonight, the boys and younger kids are in bed and the babies swaddled and fed. The house is quiet. My mother gets everything done tonight to ease the Sunday morning chaos: the chores of breakfast, feeding the babies, getting the diaper bag, and all the children ready for church.

Tonight, I am introduced into the ladies' group to put on nail polish. They have not allowed me to wear nail polish yet, and Mom tells me to give her my hand. The polish is my favorite color, bright red. The smell permeates the room, and I look around at my sisters and mother. They are laughing and complementing each other on their nails. I understand what it means to belong in the group of females. Is this how women act when they are together? It's fun, I fit in and share something with others while laughing and giggling. I guess I will tolerate those bobby pins to have curly hair. I can blow on these nails to dry them, not touching anything for the next half an hour because I am included.

This simple ritual affects me because of the shared connection and love. I lament when I miss a night because I fall asleep early and regret missing out on our bonding and sharing time together. I feel as if I've moved up – moved to the next level of grown-upness. This feeling is also a feeling of security, of being embraced by a new group without having to prove myself or give something up to belong. I am enjoying this.

Age Five; Saturday Girls' Night

I carry this yearning for sharing and acceptance for years, learning it is essential to belong. Throughout life, I indulge in connecting with my siblings and women in sharing rituals and camaraderie. It is a profound yearning for everyone to belong. These moments are significant in letting me feel what acceptance is and to search for more of it in my life. I belonged to my family of origin and shared so much happiness, connectedness, pain, and mutual love. I know in my heart what joy this brought into my life. Were these early Saturday night moments started for convenience's sake, or were they intentional? Either way, thank you, Mom.

When my heart feels love and acceptance, I recognize it immediately. I have learned to recognize groups that no longer serve me and know the difference. I notice relationships that continue to harm me or ones that nurture me, and know when to say goodbye or hello to the tribe that matches my vibe.

Ask yourself if the people in your life bring out your highest good. Do they support you in love and accept you with your defects without judging? Belonging isn't about being included; it should lift you up to be the best you can be. It can also tear you down with manipulation and false friendships. It is your choice to who and what you want to connect. Evaluate and give yourself the connections you want in your life, the ones supporting your highest self.

Age Five; Running

Innocence before and after

Unaware before . . . Happy with life as it is.

Seconds, minutes, hours, or years

Between . . . Bring you to after

The awakening, the knowing, the loss . . .

Before . . . the loss of freedom, not having to know

The after . . . Awareness . . .

My Childhood: Getting Over it

Running, running, running, I've got to pee. I've got to pee! Will I make it? Yes, I'm there! I Turn the handle, and I am removing my shorts.

My dad is in the tub, "Get out of here right now!" he yells.

"What, I've got to pee?" I respond.

He yells, "Get out!" I'm waiting, dancing, hopping, and the door opens Ahh! I can finally pee.

"What the hell is the matter with you, are you sick?" he continues. "Who the fuck told you to come in while I'm in the tub?" he asks. I back away and stare at him, naked with a towel wrapped around his waist. I have never seen him undressed or even without a shirt. My curiosity takes over me.

"You're sick, why are you staring at me?" he bellows. I recall it in my mind. His hand comes at me. I fly up against the wall and slide downward in slow motion as I wet myself. His voice brings me back. "Never do that again." he says as he goes back into the bathroom.

I don't know why he called me sick. What did I do and what just happened to me, why did it happen in slow motion? I recognized the feeling when I wet myself as pure terror. Confusion overwhelms be. How could my dad hit me that hard? What did I do that brought about such anger? I can't shake off my feelings for hours (even years) Dad has moved on from the incident and is joking with my brothers and sisters.

Age Five; Running

I can't look at him and hide out in my room for hours. Not out of fear anymore, but shame for something I can't understand yet.

I felt a loss of innocence, embarrassment, and betrayal by my dad. The message I received that day was about fear power (men) and trust. I had witnessed my dad's violence toward others, but until that day I hadn't remembered him hitting me. My confusion for the reason overwhelmed me as I connected it to my father. Who can I trust in life, people and even the universe? Where do I put my anger and embarrassment? Not knowing why, my innocence shifted. My social identity and my limited power changed who I would become and how I viewed men in the world that day. It opened my perception, made me aware of the power of men.

I also learned how terror felt in my body. What a gift. I will rely on this feeling in my lifetime and listen to it. I have known the feeling in my dreams, this fear, and it was always present. I can still recall this day and the feelings at age sixty. Releasing the roots of fear is now my biggest work.

Fear is not a bad thing or a good thing, it is a feeling. One to be aware of, because if you allow yourself to listen to it, it will show you where and what the fear represents. Honor it for its honesty, as a door, if you will, to walk through to the deeper parts of yourself.

Age Seven; Grandpa Papp's Visit

meeting him for the first time

hesitant, observing, not trusting

a stranger, after all

mustache long and curled,

eyes that twinkle and also brooding

joking to make us comfortable or himself

visiting for several months, they say

Hmmm . . . who is this grandpa?

My Childhood: Getting Over it

I grew up without grandparents, because they all lived in Hungary. Grandpa Papp, Josef, who is my dad's dad, is coming for his first visit to the United States on a visa. The three boys sleep in a room with a twin and a double bed. One of my brothers has to sleep with me in my full-size bed, and another has to sleep with Grandpa and listen to his snoring. When my grandfather goes to work with my dad, we sneak into his huge brown, pulverized suitcase. His arrival brings gifts that just keep coming out of that suitcase: candy, chocolate, clothes, and toys from Europe. The beautifully colored wind-up toys are fascinating. Pandas beating a drum, and soldiers that march when wound up with a key in their backs. The Hershey's candy bars we are familiar with do not compare to the creamy chocolates from Europe.

The brown battered satchel is now being refilled with gifts returning to Hungary. We discover several jars of peppermint chewing gum and stuff our mouths with it. My brothers and sisters return to that case throughout the day, and so do I. A few hours later, we have the worst diarrhea mom has ever seen. She frantically cleans us and tries to figure out what we ate because we do not have any other symptoms. Grandfather figures it out at once, as he goes upstairs and comes down with an empty bottle of ex-lax chewing gum. They all laugh. We don't think it's that funny, but learn never to put our trust in those Chicklet-shaped tablets again.

Another Grandpa memory during his visit involves his snoring and we children teasing him. The two brothers in the room with the snoring can't sleep, and my brother and I in my bed can't either. My brother comes up with an idea to wake our grandfather with my doll. When you tip the doll over on its stomach, it repeats "Mama" a few times. The first "Mama" sound wakes up Grandpa, who looks around trying to see where the sound is coming from. He becomes agitated af-

Age Seven; Grandpa Papp's Visit

ter waking up several times. I must admit as kids we repeat the game to overkill. We can't help ourselves and hide under the covers giggling. We don't stop laughing until he throws the blankets back and discovers the doll. My brother and I become sober at once, thinking a smack are on its way. He takes the doll back with him and throws it on the floor next to his bed with one last "Mama "cycle echoing in the next room. We laugh the next day, repeating the story to each other.

One of my grandfather's favorite hobbies is hunting, and he hunts with my dad a few times while he is visiting here. He has never seen a skunk and gets too close to one out of curiosity. When they arrive home, my mother throws his clothes out, which makes him angry. She explains that she is not putting those smelly garments in her washer. I remember the odor is so strong I taste it and try to get as far away as possible. Everyone tries to come up with a remedy to remove the odor from his skin. They talk about tomato juice and milk baths. The smell eventually goes away with some remedy that works. My granddad never stops talking about that animal that stinks so bad.

He is a stern man with a wicked temper and also a jovial side, such a replica of my dad. Grandpa is weird, I would watch him if an adult disagreed with him. He would turn all red in the face and become angry and argumentative, sometimes yelling at the person. I felt bad for the person at the other end of his tirades because it seemed their only option was to leave. After a day of fishing he would make his "famous fish soup". He would take all the eyes of the fish and put them in a small bowl, sprinkle them with a little salt and eats them. I turned my head before I saw the little eyes go into his mouth so I don't know if he really did eat them. The bowl was empty when I check back. While eating his fish soup he would throw a coughing fit as if he was choking, to demonstrate what would happen if we ate a

My Childhood: Getting Over it

fish bone. Then he would lecture us on chewing carefully, because the fish might have fish bones in them that he missed during his filleting. I don't know if it is because I don't know him, or I don't have anyone to compare him to. We do not have any aunts, cousins, or uncles living near us. My closest uncle (my mother's brother) lives in Milwaukee, and I met him once at such a young age, I only remember sleeping in the car on the way to visit him. My dad was the only male I can compare him to, and they are so alike, my grandfather always disagreeing with my dad's opinion, dismissing it with an "aye" and the wave of his hand.

Grandpa was the first person I met in my extended family. Until this point, I hadn't met or remembered meeting any uncles, aunts, grandparents, or cousins. He joked with us kids, and then, like my dad, he became argumentative when he drank. A fear of trust again rose within me.

The fear of the unknown, the anger that could explode without provocation. I continued to be on guard, listening, looking for clues and adjusting my spirit to what could happen. As I get older and listen to horror stories of my grandfather, I reconnect to my meeting him, and it's hard to bridge who I met with the violent, angry man I hear about. Yet I know it's possible because his son raised me.

I see a generational anger in this story, in a father, his son, and in my father's sons. I see how this same anger manifests in my family in distinct ways. Visible with large egos, addictions, answers through religion to control it. Mimicking family love to suppress the anger at all costs.

Age Seven; Grandpa Papp's Visit

None of the methods are successful in containing the rage.

I am consciously becoming my generation's healer in expressing anger, listening to its history, and knowing that it can heal the past and future. As my actions, patterns and beliefs transform that energy flows to those around me. My acceptance of myself radiates to my children and the souls that came before us, we are all connected and the threads of healing link us whether we are on the planet or not.

Anger held in by generations genetically changes DNA with our trauma and anger experiences by not turning on the necessary genes at the appropriate times in our physical growth. The anger produced by trauma affects our cellular growth. How can we even question it not being passed on to the next generation? Our addictions rise from our past and can be demonstrated to us by observations, feelings, and patterns. Think for a moment about your family; do you recognize any patterns? We have all heard or said, "I will never be like my dad or mom," and then as we age, we recognize our parents in ourselves. How could it NOT be? Our patterns and reactions have had years to develop and reside in our subconscious. Exploring them begins to bring them out to observe, notice and change. If you can't bring yourself to look at these patterns – how can you change them?

Age Seven; My Guitar

A child's

expectation

Reasonable

Entitled

Necessary

Doable

Expected

Dreaming

Knowing

Hope Arriving

My Childhood: Getting Over it

A child of seven still trusts in Christmas, so I asked for a guitar. Everybody knows my dream for a guitar; that's all I talk about daily. I visualize the exact feel and sound of how I will create music. Imagining my joy in performing—I just know I can master playing it with ease.

Yes, I sneak downstairs to the tree to check out the packages. The soft ones I toss aside, knowing those are from Mom and Dad and are PJs and socks. I discover the long, narrow box, ahhhh . . . my guitar. Yes, it is heavier at one end when I rattle the box because the neck end of the guitar is lighter. The package isn't exactly wide enough, I know, I know, because the guitar is a smaller child's size.

On the day of, I rip open my Christmas-themed-wrapped-awaited gift. What! A baton! Who wants a fucking baton? A stick with two rubber ends, not a toy, a tool, a sports item, or even an accessory. What the FUCK?? What a delusion, my guitar dream shattered. This was a once-a-year opportunity to maybe receive what I wanted. Asking, repeating, hoping in an effort to force my dream into a reality. Gone – for another year!

Hesitating for a moment, I glance around the room, seeing my brothers' and sisters' excitement. I also see my parents' joy in watching our excitement to stop me from blurting out, "What the FUCK! Where's my guitar?"

I play excited and thankful, and blend in with the bedlam of opening presents on Christmas morning. No one recalls my guitar ask and wish. After a while, I forget as well.

Age Seven; My Guitar

Few of my expectations reached fruition growing up, and I learned to expect little from others and the world. Not expecting much from myself, sacrificing my joy for others, was a recurring theme in my life. I lost my joy while growing up, giving it to others, hiding it like a jewel that could be stolen at any moment. I now know that my creativity brings me joy in whatever format it arrives. I have joy in the moments of living, stretching those moments into minutes, hours, and days. Practicing daily.

Tapping into my joy teaches me more about myself and shows me where I need to grow and open. When I experience my hopes and joy clashing together, I know I am in the mooment and where I should be.

Your joy is your guide to being your authentic self. Not the joy of watching others or giving others their joy. You will always feel your joy and recognize it in yourself, if only you are able will act on it. I am not talking about happiness. I am talking about joy. What's the difference?

Joy requires a connection, often with people, but can also be with pets, creation, creativity, etc. Joy is present, in the moment. It is a choice, an attitude of your heart and spirit, residing inside of us and can share its space with other emotions — sadness, shame or anger whereas happiness can't. Joy brings you peace and contentment.

When you know it's your joy, you anticipate it arriving. You will know that it is where you belong. Feeling that joy is the joy of your authentic self arriving home. A knowing that this is what you have to do. Have you felt this in your life? If you have then go back to it, explore it, go deeper into what it is that brings that up in you. this practice will allow joy to come to you.

Age Eight; Head Lice Treatment

How you hold my pain

In the deepest recesses of my brain

Poking to the surface

when

A smell, an impression, or a parallel

rises to the surface

Again

Growing, remembering

Coalescing once more

Each time touching that spot

Ouch!

I remember that

My Childhood: Getting Over it

Having head lice as a kid is quite the irritation. With all of her kids my mother's work is cut out for her. She keeps repeating the word Petro, that she needs Petro and for Dad to get it. The translation for the word was kerosene or turpentine, so Dad makes the purchase and Mom starts the disinfecting. One at a time, she saturates our heads with this Petro and uses torn-up sheets to wrap tight turbans around each of our crowns.

This is one of the few times she allows television and she lines us up on the sofa to wait. There we are, enjoying cartoons and laughing at each other's turban-sheeted heads. Our scalps tickle, but they are so tightly and thickly wrapped, we cannot reach the itch. As the tickle increases (the lice were trying to escape), the annoyance becomes unbearable as we stick our little fingers in around our head wraps. Mom comes over and slaps our hands, telling us to stop scratching. She then goes back to laundering the bedsheets, blankets, and clothes.

The treatment proceeds as we gaze at the TV. Our heads get warm during the next phase of the eradication. This warmth feels uncomfortable, combined with a prickly itch. We share our aggravation with each other and renew our attention to the show. The mild heat turns into a burning sensation, and we groan loudly complaining to mom. Mom returns to check under the turbans and reports, "Not yet," as if she's cooking something and it is not quite ready. The level of heat increases and our anguish heightens. When it becomes unendurable, we all start crying.

Mother determines that we are ready for the cleansing. Starting with the three smaller children, she removes the linen wraps. Ahhhh! My turn comes in the second wave, and she removes each layer, releasing my head from the hot vice. My skull is tingling with

Age Eight; Head Lice Treatment

numbness. With the claw-foot tub filled with warm water, she drops three of us in. She scrubs and then shampoos each head with a bar of lemon-scented-shaped soap, purchased just for this procedure. The surface of the water in the tub glimmers with rainbows, as I was part of the second batch of bathers. The warm water on my head eases the stinging numbness until Mom announces its time to get out. It takes a while for my scalp to feel normal. I cheer—I completed the ordeal. Or so I thought.

Again, starting with the youngest, Mom combs our hair with the smallest comb I've ever seen. It pulls at our hair while removing eggs from our hair shafts. She patiently combs through the girls' hair, then gives the boys a brush cut before going through their hair. Laying in her lap while she combs lasts forever until she releases us with tear-streaked faces. She checks each scalp religiously for the next week and, if deemed contaminated, we are once again forced into the combing lap.

We children discuss the various ways to catch lice and its collection of prevention methods. We vow never to use anyone's comb, touch heads with another human being, or use anyone else's hat. I don't recall ever going through this process again in the future.

What did I carry from this tribulation into adulthood? I remember the misery of this calamity and the joy of being liberated to return to childhood. I always think of this memory when I hear someone tell me they have or their grandchildren have head lice. My trust in my mother doing the right or best thing for me shifted that day. I can remember how my head felt that day, burning, numbing,

45

My Childhood: Getting Over it

and tingling. Not a good tingling, a tingling of my head awakening after trauma. I began noticing my mother's home remedies and questioned the warm, salt-filled sock placed on your ear when you had an earache. The castor oil for constipation. They could have been the cure, and yet I still questioned them. That lack of trust again rising, questioning my mother, because her cures usually meant pain was coming with it.

When the top of my head gets sunburned, my body reconnects the pain of the extermination trauma immediately. I can now reframe this experience knowing my mother did not realize the pain she caused to our heads. She used the best method she knew how to get rid of her problem. I can imagine how overwhelmed she was with all those little heads. It didn't mean she didn't love us and she had to get her world back to normal ASAP. The stigma of headlice running through the neighborhood. The cleanliness questions, the mothering questions all surrounding her, pressuring her for the fix, a fix. The best one she knew.

We can all relate to our parents being overwhelmed and reacting to a situation in their quickest and most efficient manner, not considering the long-term consequences imparted on their children. It was not done out of hate but more out of their perceived necessity? Forgiveness of parents is one of the strongest healers for yourself. The roles, pain and teachings they gave you in your life were more than what was on the surface. Your freedom to grow into who you are meant to be hinges so much on your ability to forgive them most of all and to allow your own forgiveness to show up.

Age Eight; The Swimming Pool

My body is mine

or is it

My body is beautiful

Hide it

My body is innocent

not to some

My body is safe

always be on guard

My body is female

there are rules

My body is covered

let it stay that way

My body is mine

or is it

My Childhood: Getting Over it

I am running around, jumping and screaming with my brothers and sisters, so excited about getting a swimming pool. Dad has arrived at home with a friend and an enormous box that contains a pool. We don't care how deep, how big, if it has a filter, or even how many of us will fit into it. We are out of school and have a summer pool. We stand around in anticipation while they empty the box and its contents onto the grass, in the perfect spot in the yard. They lay a tarp and instructions out on the ground. The sides of the pool are unrolled and snapped together. As the excitement builds, I say, "Yeah, it will hold us." They insert and stretch the liner. I watch Dad and his friend continue with the install. Next plastic rim pieces go around the entire pool to hold the liner in place. We wait, I wait.

It is ready to hold water. Apu pulls up a chair, puts the hose in the swimming pool, and so we watch. Dad lights up as we hop around in a frenzy, teasing us about how cold the water will be. As it fills with water, my brothers undress, taking off their shoes, socks, and shirts. I am eight and follow suit; we do not own bathing suits.

While jumping with my brothers, my dad tells me to put my blouse back on. I yell back to him that my brothers don't have theirs on. He tells me again to put my shirt on. I look at my chest and exclaim "I don't need to because I don't have boobs!" My father walks over and slaps me across the face. My blouse goes back on and the magic of the moment disappears.

In one minute, I am safe, free, and unconscious of my body. In the next, I am processing why I can't be free with my body. I wasn't aware of my other sisters, their outfits, or their elation. I am reveling in my world of joy, freedom, and anticipation in plunging into the cool water and splashing.

Age Eight; The Swimming Pool

Am I different because I am a girl? Why do I have to cover up?

The memory lives, as it was the first time someone took notice of my body. Attention to my body, my female frame. I had to cover up. How does my body enter this scenario, I ask? Why? My first body consciousness and the rules of society. Cover up—be responsible for your difference, you are female. The slap representing the hard/harsh rule. I felt the anger surrounding that rule and a sense of unfairness. My child's mind records it and transforms my perception of my body and the rules that control it. My awareness of society's rules and brainwashing young girls into molds. How does society allow these messages to continue and tell our daughters they are less than?

I now know my body is mine and mine alone. It is I who chooses with whom and when to share it, hide it, manage it. I consciously refuse to accept society's rules on how it should look and why. There are plenty of rules: how it should age, dress age appropriately, shame surrounding our female bodies, intimidation, words and actions with "less than" messages. I am me and my body is mine, I will honor it for all it does for me and has done for so many years.

I challenge you to accept your body and understand the work it has done for you. Healing you in ways you are unaware of. Your body has been your most loyal partner, keeping you bound to the earth in all its magical moments. Your body discovering and feeling joy, passion, and transformation and also your reactions to the earths wonderous sunrises, sunsets and the magical moments of hearing the wind rush through the trees or smelling the rain on the pavement on a hot summer day. Staying with you through your physical battles, overindulgences, addictions, and more. Thank you, I love you, my body.

Age Eight;
The Missing Toe

As I see your pain

Empathy rises in me

My heart opens wide

My Childhood: Getting Over it

Whenever we go anywhere, we always share bikes. Sometimes three of us ride, one on the handlebars, one on the back fender, while the oldest or biggest peddles in the driver's seat. When the smaller ones want to come along, they sit on the bumper.

On this sunny summer day, my three-year-old sister Anika comes with us to the store. Anika sits on the back fender and off we ride. Eager to join, she doesn't put on her shoes and is barefoot. Before we make it to the end of the street, she screams. Her foot is bleeding profusely. My older sister picks her up and carries her home to Mom. My mother realizes that her large toe is missing and calls a friend to take them to the hospital. Before they can leave, another neighbor is at the door with Anika's little digit in a napkin. She says, "They might be able to reattach it, if you take it with you."

Someone notifies my dad at work. The rest of the family stays home, wondering if it was possible to reattach the little appendage. We ask each other, "Can they sew it on and how will it look?" We rehash the accident and the appendage conversations last until Dad comes home and tells us the toe was too jagged to sew back on. He says Anika has to stay in the hospital for a while because her foot needs surgery.

We wait anxiously for Anika to return. When the day comes, our morbid curiosity is snatched from us because they wrapped her foot in yards of gauze. We are expecting to see the damage and the space where her toe used to be. She cannot walk without help and hops from one piece of furniture to another. On the day, my mother changes her bandage. We gather around the bed to watch and ask our gruesome questions as Mom unravels the ace bandage. The smell of the dressing wafts around me, reminding me of the nurse's office at

Age Eight; The Missing Toe

school. This unwrapping procedure goes on forever, Mom continuing the unraveling around and around Anika's foot. Finally, she removes the last bloody square piece of gauze; there, her little chubby foot missing a toe, with a pointed piece of hard skin poking out of where her large toe used to be. Anika's cute little round face gazes at her foot to investigate her injury. She looks confused, not understanding her loss. Seeing Anika's little foot without a toe amazes me because it looks like a small foot missing one digit. How else could it look. It's what I expected and yet it wasn't because a foot should have five toes. I was too young to process the vision. I was waiting to see something grotesque and it wasn't.

I go to touch it, and Mom slaps my hand, telling me to let it heal. Mom cleans and rewraps the foot and a few days later forces my sister to walk without help.

During her painful rehab, we watch as she cries while being forced to walk. Banding together, we yell at Mom. "Stop hurting her, you are being so mean.". Our mother replies back, "she have to do this for her good, it vill get better, the more she valk." As she continues her torture, mom chides Anika along softly repeating, "von more step, honey, von more."

My little sister learns to walk without a limp. That painful rehabilitation with Mom's persistence gave her a normal stride. I witnessed a knowledge of having to go through a discomfort and not around it. A great prescription for moving forward is pushing through the suffering. As a child I remember, thinking about Anika's pain and her staying over in the hospital and how scared she must have

My Childhood: Getting Over it

been. Her tears during her rehab, bought up all my hero feelings of helping and alleviating pain from others. Fixing the hurt. My mother's experience forced my sister to walk through her pain over and over again to heal.

Moving through life's painful moments is the best way to heal. Not just moving through, but feeling as you move through. Sensing the depth of the pain and learning the purpose of it can bring forgiveness, acceptance, and a powerful life perspective. Feel the pain heal the pain.

Yes, it's hard, yes, crying hurts even more than a physical bruise. The release of the pain through crying, writing, creating, getting it out of your body begins the healing, and then the pain morphs. Transforms into an energy that heals and brings with it such understanding and insight. And yes, it gets easier the more you do it. I have asked my therapist, "When will I stop weeping, damn it?" She always answers, "When you are done, my dear, when you are done." Are you willing to go through the pain to get to the other side? The other side that lets you look back and say, "I survived, transformed, and healed a part of me."

Age Eight; Nicks with Dad

Individual

time with a parent

cherished hours

eternally

fixed in the mind

time passes

memory canonized

for a moment

long ago

unaware

of your knighthood

your angelic status

in the memory

of your child

My Childhood: Getting Over it

Nick Tahoe's in Rochester, New York, is an institution. In my young life, Nick's is where I go with my dad, with no brothers or sisters tagging along. Just me and him. We get off the bus before downtown, and we go into this shabby diner with a counter and stools that twirl. There is nothing fancy in the place, and Dad orders me a red hot with everything, extra hot sauce. The hot sauce is a spicy, greasy meat topping that soaks into the hot dog bun and makes the bottom bread fall apart. It is a challenge finishing this tasty mess without having your fingers smell like onions and hot sauce when finished.

I revel in the experience of having my time with Dad and getting a grown-up red hot with hot sauce that I can handle. Dad jokes with me about the mess I'm making while I twirl around the stool. He engages the customers around us in joking with him. He seems to know the owners and is talking to everyone there. After saying goodbye, we continue on with the day's errands, just me and him. We go to the bank, utility company to pay the bill, and his next stop is in a building I am unfamiliar with.

We enter a room filled with smoke where men are sitting around tables, some of them playing cards. My dad talks with them for a while as the room draws my attention away from the conversation. Men only, smoking, drinking, talking, and laughing. The smell of cigars permeates my senses, in a good way. I am with my dad as he is greeted by his first name as he walks through the room, laughing and joking. I have never seen my father so cordial and entertaining outside the family. It is fun to witness and be a part of this new experience.

Our last stop before heading home is the grocery store where dad shops and I get a sweet treat, with more joking from my dad about my teeth rotting out of my head.

Age Eight; Nicks with Dad

Riding home on the bouncing bus, I recognize the familiar landmarks that settle me into comfort and then sadness as the day with my dad is coming to an end.

Even now whenever I'm in Rochester, I go to Nick's to be with my dad in my memory. I order a red hot with everything, with extra hot sauce, and truly enjoy it. These trips that cost so little, give me a big, warm feeling and memory. Time alone spent with either of my parents as a child was such an enormous treat for me. It was during these precious few times that my image and memories of them changed, and I felt I knew them. Letting go of the distracted, angry, frustrated parent, and seeing a glimpse of their authentic selves. Their gentle, humorous and kind side that was for a moment shared with only me.

These funny, gentle references balance the awareness of my childhood. It is these glimpses of my parents without responsibilities, interruptions, and imperfections that showed me their most gentle, funny sides. They were neither all of either side. Just as we are not only the dark, bad, temperamental person all the time. We are all made up of conflicts, of the light and dark sides. Neither one being better than the other, both just opposites of each other that let us feel, portray, and act on situations in different modalities.

The harsher memories are the ones that usually stay with us. It takes work to see the human side of an abuser, a lost parent or sibling. If you can, allow the barrier to open and allow a bit of light to enter and shine within you. Dare yourself to begin the healing. Allowing in the smallest of those good memories begins to give you the image of their soul and can balance your beliefs in who they are or were.

Age Eight; Green House on Texas Street

Instincts . . . built in us

Oh, that feeling in your gut

Listen to it . . . now!!

My Childhood: Getting Over it

My mother sends me up to the corner bakery to get bread. Yes, it's safe, only fifteen houses up the same narrow, residential street we live on and then across a small intersection. Skipping toward the end of the road, I hear birds chirping, feel the sun's warmth, and I am free to be a child of eight daydreaming as I go.

Halfway to the store, a boy my age stops me and asks me if I want to play with his puppy. I pause for only a second and follow him up to his porch. I have passed this dark-colored house so many times—the peeling dark green paint and the worn-out porch, the curtains always closed. However, I have never spotted this child outside playing. Hmm . . . He opens the front door and again I hesitate. Seeing the dog overrides my hesitation in entering and then facing my mother's anger if she finds out that I stopped to play. Mom won't allow us to have pets; she says they are dirty. We walk through the entrance and down a narrow hall; the drapes are all closed, and the house is dark. The little boy's mom is in the kitchen, she stops to turn around and look at me, and says nothing. I am looking for the pup, and the boy says it's in the cellar. I pause now for the third time.

The basement stairs are dark and creepy, so I question why someone keeps a pup in the cellar? We start down the stairs and pictures of nude women cover both sides of the stair walls. I process this. Wow, so many pictures. Why are they naked, and why did this boy's dad tape them on the wall like wallpaper? I'm thinking these are pages of that magazine one of my brothers brought home one time and Mom got upset and threw it away. For a few moments, I am hypnotized by the nudity and all the distinct breasts and nipples.

Age Eight; Green House on Texas Street

As we near the bottom of the stairs, I spot a compact room across from the bottom step with a cot. I feel frightening dread, as if something horrible is about to happen to me, when out of the edge of my view I see the boy's dad. He is standing off to the left, waiting for me to step down. I run up the steps so fast I trip, regaining my balance. I go on running past the mom and out the front door.

I don't stop running until I'm home. My mom asks me where the bread is. I say nothing and race upstairs to my room. She never questions me, comes up to my room to check on me, or asks me what's wrong. I didn't understand the subtle clues (hesitations) and gut feelings leading to the basement.

I did recognize the instinct to flee and the understanding of fear and unknowing.

I don't recognize the meaning behind each trigger, and yet I do eventually run. The child never crosses my path again, not even at school. Whenever I walk toward that end of the street, I cut across to the other side to avoid getting near the green house. My brothers and sisters cross with me, never questioning or knowing why.

This story could have ended differently, had I not seen the father, the cot, and the nude pictures that triggered an internal alarm. I now think of the world that boy and his mom lived in. What happened to them? Were other girls lured to the basement? Were my sisters baited? Did the child become what his dad was exposing him to? Did the mother ever reconcile her part or release herself from this man? I escaped becoming a victim that day, and still I recognized three victims in

My Childhood: Getting Over it

this story.

Only the universe knows the answers to these questions. I don't know why the interconnectedness in writing this story resonates in my spirit. Why did I pass through their lives? As a youth, I saw a mother broken, a father overtaken by perversion, and an young son caught between this despair. Why did I need to encounter that? I believe there are no coincidences, and this incident appeared for a reason. I may never realize the answer to the question, though the memory stays with me.

I have encountered lost characters, performing unthinkable acts on themselves and others. My sentiments toward these individuals are my awareness of their life's desires. Their decisions and choices as souls for the experiences they want in their journey as a human on the earth (the teaching planet). Addicts, murderers, pedophiles, priests, nurses, doctors, and your average Jane, all longing to experience life. Creating soul pacts with others prior to birth. Leaving the route and manner it manifests to the universe (God). Never remembering this pact after their birth delivery and then living it. What are you living?

I allow myself to offer understanding and love to all I encounter on my passage through earth. It is hard, and at times I stumble and cannot give unconditional love. Just like many of you, I cannot say I'll get there in this life. I can strive toward it and continue in the next lifetime. However, it's the endeavor that will bring me closer to unconditional love not only for myself and all I encounter on my path. Love, Love, Love.

Age Eight; Pee Pie Revenge

Feelings of anger rise,

revenge for unfairness,

being used,

lied to,

brothers willing to plot,

my heart meddles,

anger retreats,

I let her go,

surprised I say

That was easy??????

My Childhood: Getting Over it

Playing with Barbies is enjoyable, with a friend, and another girl, even though you don't know her well. She lives across the street; I think she has an older brother, and she brings her Barbies to visit mine. Her mother makes most of her doll clothes. I collect and guard my outfits from my younger sisters and can identify each outfit, including shoes. When my playmate steals one of my dolls' outfits, I question myself for losing it. After the second time it happens, I confront her, and she denies taking the dresses. I am so pissed that she didn't admit to stealing them, knowing she was the only other person besides me that plays with them. I realize I'm not getting them back. I go to my brothers to bitch, and they came up with a plan of vengeance. They understand my frustration and organize a plot to teach the little theif a lesson in messing with their sister and her Barbies.

Out of sight behind the garage, they dig a hole and pee in it, making the soil muddy. The mud reeks of pee; they tell me to invite my friend over to play and bring her to them. I walk across the street to her house, pumped up, ready to get ruthless. It confuses her when I want to play again after our last exchange, but she follows me. I tell her my dolls are behind the garage. Once there, she hesitates again and then continues. My brothers surround her ordering her to eat the mud pies they made. They can hurt an outsider to get even for my hurt, showing family loyalty and unity. We must stick together. The horror expressed on her face brings me back to my kindhearted senses, as I slap the pie out of my brother's hand. I tell her I have changed my mind on playing with our dolls, and she runs home, avoiding the boys' nasty pies and wrath. She never comes over to play with me again.

Age Eight; Pee Pie Revenge

I feel full of vengeful anger one minute and then feel pity the next. This is the first time I recall having such an abrupt change of emotions for someone else outside the family. The look on that girl's face touches my heart, and my notions of vengeance slip away.

Even today I can consider retribution after I am hurt by someone. The closer their relationship to me, the stronger the feelings. I recognize that the revenge, in whatever form, will not take away my hurt. I fantasize about pretending that I would not recognize someone when they see me and say hi at the mall or store, letting them know how insignificant they were in my life. So, take that will you!! Developing a pattern of silence to punish was imbedded in me. I read about holding space in my head (rent) for those who have hurt me and how freeing and healing it is to let them go for my well-being, and to incorporate that new philosophy in my heart as much as my engrafted pattern allows.

Vengeance is no longer in my repertoire. Just as I cannot command another, I can manage my reaction to their malice toward me. I no longer allow unnecessary, hurtful people to rent space in my head. I choose to open that space to goodness and no longer allow it to remain there roosting, churning, and cluttering my space.

How does vengeance control your life? Will the satisfaction you crave with this retribution fall flat? Try it, or look back to a time you carried out your repayment. Was it gratifying, was it short-lived, did it carry you higher? A great teaching tells us that reaction is always about the past. Don't you want to live in the present?

My Childhood: Getting Over it

I also must comment on clan loyalty. Even at eight, I could count on my brothers defending me. The family loyalty that was demonstrated, encouraged, and talked about by my parents. It will take a tremendous journey later in life to examine this allegiance and what that means to me. Does loyalty supersede hurtful situations? Is this loyalty stronger than the loyalty to yourself? Do your family or friends ask or require you to give up parts of yourself for the loyalty of the whole? What is that cost your authenticity?

Age Nine; The Dairy

being present

as a child

only using boundaries

we are aware of

joining dirt heedlessly

time passing, unconcerned

joyful fun, banter and camaraderie

making choices

actions, friends, and precedent

observing and absorbing

all that is in between

Absent parental supervision

getting hurt, moving on

rules of play, rules of life

perceptions get blurred

My Childhood: Getting Over it

We live alongside a dairy and use a well-worn path through the yard. We cut through to reach Lyell Avenue, which is the primary thoroughfare leading to the world. The avenue is busy with foot and street traffic, having many types of businesses: a laundromat, the big grocery store, the drugstore, the dentist, the butcher, and so much more. We can't keep out of the adventurous yard and consider it our playground. The dairy has an abandoned milk truck from the forties in the back-parking lot. Milk crates in the lot piled twenty feet high in rows and columns. Year-round access to an ice silo full of shaved ice that is available for play.

All the delivery trucks pull up to the silo before starting their daily routes, filling their vans with ice. What fun to have snowball wars in the middle of the summer! We fill up crates with these balls and take them to Lyell Avenue to throw at the buses and cars. Regrettable for you if you have your window rolled down. The competition among each other is to get the icy globe into the open windows as the cars drive by. We high-five and laugh at the drivers' faces when they realize a snowball hit them in the heart of summer.

We build castles deep within the crates with adjoining rooms. Expanding my imagination as I spend hours building, creating, only to find the fort destroyed the next day. An ancient man at the dairy chases us from these forts. He reports our unruliness to our Mom saying for safety's sake, keep your children out of there. Mom does not discourage our play as we are out of the house, enjoying the sun. Our adventures in the dairy yard keep us busy all summer long. We play unsupervised all day, enacting stories, pretending we are driving, married, builders, secret agents and more. Checking in for lunch, sometimes forgetting. We wait for the last car in the dairy yard to leave before we begin our games.

Age Nine; The Dairy

One of the finest rewards of living next to this play yard is the free dairy products we gather after the trucks return from their daily runs. The large green dumpsters hold all the dairy we can handle. Mom encourages her children to dive in and retrieve the unspoiled items. We climb out with white liquid dripping from our legs as we bring the booty back home. Mom smells each container before making butter and whipped cream out of the heavy cream. Chocolate drink is in abundance.

Mom's zeal in baking with this treasure of daily products expands. It is fun for us, except for getting all milked up in the dumpster and the old guy waving his stick, scaring us out of the huge, green treasure chest. after much haggling we designate a lookout, which is a comparatively cushy job. The lookout does not have to take part in the messy milk retrieval process and also gets the quickest and furthest away from the old fellow with the stick. The cat-and-mouse game plays out throughout the summer. And as the summer ends, the elder with the stick uses a little of his wisdom and begins to puncture the cartons before dumping them in the dumpster. However, he manages to miss a few quarts of milk from each crate he dumps. Knowing we will continue our dumpster diving; he is appeasing both the dairy managers and our need for the family milk.

I recall so much fun playing in that dairy. I don't remember pausing to eat during the summer days, and surely, I must have. We would play for hours, secluded in the stacks of milk crates, studying society's social structures with other kids, rules, what alienates friends, and what actions form friendships.

My Childhood: Getting Over it

It was a hit-or-miss school as the hits imbedded into your conscious and the misses relegated to the unconscious to create beliefs and patterns.

It was all about how to interact, negotiate, and fit into a societal group. Learning what you will compromise and what you won't to get along and still maintain playmates for tomorrow. With no supervision, we are on our own, learning how to fit in and follow along. It was all trial and error, driven by the basic need of belonging. These interactions shaped my theories of who I should be and also gave me models of who I preferred to be attracted to.

I have repeatedly wondered if others do the same with me. Do they size me up by my physical appearance, my words, clothes, etc.? I no longer care if they do, and is it a pattern we all develop to fit in. Our first instinct is to examine if this is the right person, or group for me; do you, they measure up? Look into the eyes of these people and see them, their souls, and you will understand they are in your group, the human group. Have you looked into the eyes of someone during an entire conversation? Why not? You will learn more about yourself from the eyes of others than you might expect. You will connect and be much more willing to accept your sameness versus your differences.

Children adapt to their recognition of ordinary. The dumpster diving was fun and games. We ate the meals my mother made with the rubbish with glee, only knowing that they tasted great. It changed our perception of trash and our routine. Is drinking and eating food from a dumpster okay and or even acceptable? Normal changes in access and needs. Our observations as children as our mother prepared desserts out of the waste did not go unnoticed. However, we enjoyed the adventures and the rewards.

Age Nine; The Dairy

I try to be open to the nonnormal when it shows up in my life. Needs and opportunities show up all around us daily. Observing these connections is a practice. Being able to watch others struggle and recognize it is a beautiful gift; acting on it is what takes you to another level. I am more sensitive as an adult because of these childhood experiences. I remember and recognize the body language, facial expressions, of hunger and the hesitation in other's nonreactions for help. When they say they are not hungry and it is lunch time, because they cannot pay for their lunch.

Children are observant by nature and recognize needs, sadness, and pain in others. How do we grow out of this? Can you return to your childhood gift of observation? Hmm. Recognizing what lacks in others requires you to take your attention off yourself and see others. Many times, the opportunity arises for a moment—acknowledge and take action in these moments, and your life will change.

Age Nine; Mom Quits Smoking

Thunder

Crashing clatter

broken china scattered

asshole, how can you be so cruel

Broken

My Childhood: Getting Over it

Mom quits smoking Kent Kings and purchases a giant piggy bank that she places on top of the refrigerator so we can't reach it. She puts change in the bank when she has it for every pack of cigarettes she no longer buys. She raids the pig from time to time for grocery items, but mostly she keeps filling that enormous pink grinning pig until one day it's just about full.

The day she empties it is a big day, she's going to McCurdy's to buy a twelve-piece china set. She has been talking about this set for months, about the pretty pink flower rose pattern. When she arrives home, unpacking, I observe as she washes every item and then fills the dining hutch. The pink rose pattern is beautiful, and each piece has gold trimmed edges. She is so proud of her chinaware.

In the years that follow, I study her as she entertains with that china and uses her pieces whenever she invites parishioners from church. This set replaces a mismatch of the rummage sale china she put together through the years. Her guests praise her cooking, and she loves how her meals look in her rose-rimmed receptacles, a vessel or plate to hold each entrée, soup, salad, and side.

Forward to a few years later, during a vicious argument between my parents. I'm upstairs trying to hide from the rampage, and I hear a colossal crashing of glass, sounding like all the windows in the house breaking at once, and then a hushed stillness and silence follows. I creep down the stairs to find mom in the dining room on her knees crawling around an overturned dining cabinet, picking up fragments of her broken china. After stacking the few items that did not break, I help her right the cabinet to see if any plates survived.

Age Nine; Mom Quits Smoking

I look at her, holding back tears as she sweeps up the shattered glass.

I know what the set means to her and watch how she handles her cherished dishes, bowls and her emotions

I have a hard time justifying Dad's actions, no matter how angry he is. The entire family knows the story behind the chinaware buy and how proud my mother is of her tableware, including my father. He has left the house, leaving mom to pick up the fragments. I wonder what made him so angry to visit this much breakage onto my mother.

My mom keeps those few unbroken pieces until the day she dies. As I age and am served a plate with food Mom has lovingly prepared, the image of my mother on her knees picking up her broken china resurfaces. Will this picture ever leave my mind? Probably not, but my feelings around it will heal. This incident shaped my belief in saving and spending money on pleasant things for myself. I also recognize this pattern in my siblings, instead of physically fighting, we would break each other's possessions and toys to cause pain or to seek revenge.

Yes, this experience taught me to save and also not to, because eventually you lose what you save for. The violence surrounding this episode put a fear around money in my brain. I now know that these beliefs are not true, and I don't fear saving. I have taken the old beliefs and changed them by going into this tragedy and how it affected my internal belief. Sitting with the beliefs and feelings behind them shifted my thinking.

My Childhood: Getting Over it

I hope you too will go back to your money stories and examine how you think about them and whether those beliefs are still accurate today? Do you continue to carry those assumptions? How are they no longer true for you? Explore? There is more than enough for you. You do not have to give up, hoard up, or fear success. Your money beliefs come from your past. Can you remember? Have you ever explored your money beliefs?

Age Nine; Chiller

I play "Chiller" while growing up on a narrow city street, called Texas Street.

A hide and seek game, naming the seeker, "the Chiller" to incite a feeling of fear

We create the boundaries, determine the Chiller by employing a rhyme and our feet.

You'll join him in his hunt, if you let yourself get caught.

Jumping fences, sheltering behind garbage cans, running till the performers are silent.

Excitement, fear, sweat, and adrenaline coursing through my body.

The exillerating smell of grass and earth when my face hits the ground.

Never able to depend on the trust of another player to tell me the truth,

Swearing the Chiller hasn't touched him.

And then, shit, I'm it

Seeking, calling out, scouting for movement, who can I seize, who can I lure?

It's dark; it's always dark when the Chiller goes hunting.

My Childhood: Getting Over it

Ah, there's someone over behind that moving bush.

The chase takes off, I stumble, I fall, no time to react, keep running

I must catch someone else to transfer the Chiller cloak.

No, I swear, "I'm not it anymore, Les got caught, he's the Chiller now!"

No, "I haven't seen him since we started running."

"Sucker, you fell for it!" I shout, "Ooou, ooot." Echoes throughout the neighborhood.

Everybody reassembles and a new Chiller cycle starts after the count to twenty

With clothes ripping, knees and elbows bleeding, I never give up until Mom calls.

I hope for the next opportunity to play again, when enough players gather.

Is it the fear, or the pure bliss of being a kid and abandoning life's rules?

Those nights of excitement live within me and will never wane.

I love this poem/story because I still feel the adrenaline pumping as I write about it. I remember jumping over fences, running, getting out of breath, and feeling so alive as a child during this game.

Age Nine; Chiller

No boundaries, physically or in my spirit. Enjoying the game, laughing, hiding, and sharing with the players.

Taking in the smells around me as if I was a part of them. Smelling the grass as I hit the ground with my face when running and then getting up without suffering the pain.

It is our childhood memories that can bring our aliveness back to us. How do we recapture that intensity? Shared energy, being present, with the players of life, laughing. Yes, the answer is joy. Pure joy: find it, play with it, laugh with it, and reclaim it.

I challenge you to find that delight. To close your eyes and hold it deeply as if in an imagery meditation. What are the smells, tastes, senses that come to you? Bring those sensory images back with you into the present and continue to sense them. Allow yourself to feel joy and abandonment. Your childhood pains and joys holds the answers to your destiny.

Age Ten; Popping Canning Jars

Pop, pop, pop

Observing jars

preserves that will now rot

A curious boy just being a boy

Mom's reaction to her hard work

Canned fruits

Exposed to air

Holding back

And not letting loose

on that curious boy

saving him

saving the fruit

My Childhood: Getting Over it

My mother cans fruit during the summer, while she collects all kinds of glass jars. Dad takes us to the local farms to pick peaches, cherries, pears, and plums. Not being able to afford to replace the metal lids every year, she improvises. Mom knows how important the glass is, and so she saves all shapes and sizes, boils them, fills them with fruit and boiled syrup. Necessity being the mother of invention, she takes three to four layers of Saran wrap, cuts them into squares, places them on top of the jars, and stretches rubber bands tightly around the mouth of the glass to hold the wrap onto the glass container. During the boiling process, the wrap tries its darndest to escape, and it makes an airtight domed seal on top of each jar. The jars will grow fungi if the seal is not tight or if the wrap bubbles up over the rubber band.

Hundreds of vessels line the shelves in the canning room. The volume of fruit my Mother prepares amazes me. On a rainy day, we play in the basement around a huge, coal furnace. One of my brothers enters the canning room. He has a rusty nail from the workbench and begins to pop the domed lids. I yell at him as I run up the steps to alert Mom. My mother comes to the basement and sees the many tattered Saran wrap coverings. She goes through the room, collecting the jars, shaking her head. She gently chastises my brother, explaining that the open tops make the fruit rot.

My brother does not realize what he is doing and only enjoys the noise of the popping when he pierces the wrapped lids. I witness my mother's setback in her lost labor, her quick response in saving the fruit as we eat the contents of the open jars in as many different forms as mom can conjure up.

Age Ten; Popping Canning Jars

I watch my brother's delight in listening to the sound of popping and see his dread in understanding he is in trouble. Not realizing why, and then my mom's gentle explanation and reprimand.

Children witness much in life, and this brief incident stays with me for years. The capacity of observation and how one learns arrives subtly and stays until we need it. As I witness my brother's joy and simple pleasure for entertainment, I also knew its consequences. The destruction to an adults labor and how she understands a child and reacts to this loss with tenderness to a youngster's reckless curiosity.

The interactions between a mother and a child are weighty. Each infusing energy toward the other, mirroring and reacting as humans. Both souls experiencing faults, learning, growing, and failing. The experiences burying a seed, consciously and unconsciously, into our souls. I can grow from this memory by remembering gentleness toward my child, even though they are now grown. I will try and put aside my own labor (in life) to let gentleness enter. To let love, enter into my reactions of their unawareness.

Move outside of your family to remember those seeds. Have they grown and/or are they wanting to sprout and shoot toward the sun? Shed light on those seeds, water them with tears, let the learning grow from you. It's easy to look back and also stay in the present as you observe from a distance. Treat others awareness with a gentle spirit.

Age Ten; Church Candy Fundraising

Excited at first

getting tired of it fast

wanting to go home

My Childhood: Getting Over it

Have you ever been part of a parish or school fund raising? It can start out fun until an adult drives it to an extreme record, breaking personal best goal that offers his children up with it. My dad's excitement expects his children to take on an adult work energy. The parishioners start a drive to produce cash to install carpeting (not sure, but whatever it was, we needed it). On Saturday, Dad drives the Volkswagen bus filled with cartons of candy and kids—heck we have at least four that were old enough. Another family has at least that many. For a few hours, we walk the streets, going from house to house. Repeating our little pitch on why we are raising the funds and our organization. I appeal to them to buy a can of Katydids, chocolate Covered Cherries, or Turtle Clusters. My Dad is a deacon and comes forward to help raise money for the cause (carpet, pews???). After a few weeks, he receives praise and acknowledgment for his efforts (and ours). My father then doubles his endeavors.

The selling excursions advance into a mini business model. The other family has dropped out of the fundraising drive. Dad drops his children at the corner of a street and meets us at the opposite end when we finish. He instructs us that if we run out of candy, to locate him at the end of the street to get more inventory. Dad tells us to remember the house we stopped at so we can resume sales after we reload with stock, and so a process is now in place. Merchandising by myself means I no longer have an ally to pass the time with or help me make the sale. I pray for rainy days; it was the only hindrance that stops sales because it damaged the goods. My fingers turn numb during the colder days. The sun sets, and that two-toned, red-and-white VW bus is nowhere in sight.

Ringing doorbells and waiting for answers makes me uptight. I wonder if the customer will buy. People get upset at me for disrupting

Age Ten; Church Candy Fundraising

their evening, for making them rise from their sofa, for marketing a religion that isn't theirs, and for the tins being so expensive. As they open the storm doors, the warmth and smell of their homes rushes out. I take in the front room and the heated comfort within, wishing I was home in my socks. People invite me in as they retrieve money. I stand there getting warm while whoever is in the living room stares or asks questions regarding the candy, the faith, or the weather. It exposes me to a few perverse men who greet me with lecherous smiles and ask where my parents are? The streets run on forever, and I never run out of candy.

My Dad comes up with a way to make a larger profit after he spots an end cap of chocolate-covered cherries marked for clearance at a local drugstore. These packages are one-fourth the cost he is paying the fundraising company. He sticks our churches' sticker on the cartons and off we go, tripling the profits in a few days. The pastor's wife receives phone calls from customers telling her the cherries sold to them have small white worms in them. She promptly calls the fundraising organization to report the quality of product they are supplying. The supplier demands to see the expiration dates on his cartons and, yes, it's discovered that the church stickers are on drug store boxes and not his brand. My dad's intentions are in the right place. But the candy contractor demands restitution for the smudge on his reputation and refuses to supply the congregation with any added shipments.

After this fiasco, Dad attempts to get more inventory. He knows he made a mistake but is still eager to continue with the fundraising. He has a plan to go directly to the distributor, and I go with him. After a large, older gentleman refuses to fill another order, he struggles to display respect toward my persistent, aggressive father. The man remains polite and refuses to give into my father's demands

My Childhood: Getting Over it

and verbal assaults. I watch as my dad struggles with the loss of his heroism, because I have also seen the pastor and parishioners congratulate and encourage his venture during and after church services. He has surpassed the set goal and is now working on replacing another necessary item for the church.

At church, parishioners stare at me, swaying their heads. I don't connect this admonition to the candy fiasco because the stares and head shaking occur often when it involves the wild Papp kids. No more selling (begging) people to buy overpriced tins of sweets. Days of marketing until dark are over. Ah, the simple choice to stay at home, to read a book or play a game with my brothers and sisters. Feeling warm with my socks on, being ten.

To this day, I always buy candy from kids selling it. Yes, we learned what work ethic was, helping a cause, and yet those days were not enjoyable. The selling was exhausting with no end in sight. I learned that different work ethics existed between individuals. As adults, we can forget that children are just that, children. Our excitement can overpower a child's limited energy and ability to grasp the concept we are trying to teach them. I remember wanting to go back to being a kid.

I have learned to be a child as an adult, to dance, sing, and joke lightheartedly. Responsibility no longer means excluding fun. My spontaneous laughter at one's attempt to maintain control is not as judgmental as it is entertaining. Today I enjoy the company, energy, and impulses of my grandchildren with abandon, trying diligently to not imart my adult expectations onto them, letting them rise to their own age appropriate abilities and responses.

Age Eleven; Fifty-Cent Food Coupons

I have to tell myself (out loud) that trying to control other's situations is an illusion. The more you practice letting it happen, the closer you will get to being in that child's place of joy so everything unravels as it should. Listen to your internal dialogue as it unfolds. What are you telling yourself? Can you laugh at it? Try! How hard do you work? Are you working to work; to avoid; as an addiction? Are you enjoying it, or do you too want to flee? What is your work ethic and where did it come from? Is it serving you or are you serving it?

Age Eleven;
Fifty-Cent
Food Coupons

Government issue

Always chaperoned by scams

Cravings Justified

My Childhood: Getting Over it

Back in the late sixties, food stamps (coupons) arrive in colourful booklets. Each denomination leaflet is a specific color and denomination. Fifty-cents is the smallest group of coupons. I watch Mom pay for groceries with these multicolored bills as she struggles to rip them out of their stapled booklets. My mother holds up the grocery line by taking pains to count the correct number of tens, fives, and fifty cents. Eyes roll behind and ahead as the cashier apologizes to patrons. In shame, we cluster around Mom, helping load the cart, counting and detaching the sticky dollars. The urgency to flee the embarrassment speeds up our ability in solving these math exercises. The judging eyes around us and our red cheeks disappear as we pass the gumball machines near the exit. I move Mom along to blend into the world. It is during these checkouts I observe that if the change returned is under fifty cents, you pick up the difference in coins. Cash coins.

Hmm . . .

My brothers and I consider the coupon rules, and we devise a trial trip to confirm our theory. We sneak into the house and hurriedly tear out a fifty-cent coupon from the booklet in Mom's purse. We run up to Star Market, and search the aisles for a five-cent package of unsweetened Kool-Aid, because we have determined it is the cheapest item in the store. I stride forward and approach a young cashier versus the older, grumpy-looking woman. I hand the young, smiling teen the fifty-cent coupon, and she tells me we cannot rip the coupon from the booklet before payment. I look at her with the most guiltless expression I can muster and mumble, "My mom didn't want to give me the whole book." She lets it go this time, but she says, "Tell your mom the rule." I stand by as the drawer opens with the pack of Kool-Aid in my hand. And yes! She is making change for forty-five cents with no hesitation. The transaction goes smoothly now that we are armed with

Age Eleven; Fifty-Cent Food Coupons

the rules. Still, we always look around to make sure no one we know is around to see us use the coupons.

Another money-making program is born. Forty-five cents is forty-five cents to a child. My mom is always misplacing the fifty-cent coupon booklets, or so she thinks. I approach the crabby old cashier who gives us a scan but honors the transaction. My brothers and I go to separate stores and mirror the buy, and we create a practice. One of us moves through one line at the store, then passes the booklet on to another, and he proceeds through his line.

The petty pleasures we buy with that change are thrills I don't normally get. I am justified and proud of our hustle. I enjoy those candy bars, hostess cupcakes and pop more because of the success of our coupon scam. We made it happen, yes, we thought it through, strategized, perfected it and are enjoying the fruits of our ingenious labor.

This hustle rose to accommodate a lack we had as children. We designed a system to get what we thought was a deserved treat. The government provided us with a program we took advantage of. The mind is always aware and creating to fulfill a lack, craving, or hunger. Children are little humans with a developing intellect. How natural to form a plan to fulfill a perceived need.

I want to continue to experience my inventiveness as needs arise and know that I can still figure out a dilemma and develop a process to take care of it. My maturity can now be my guide to the ethics and honesty I can incorporate into any of my actions. This confidence in my ability to process is so implanted in my adult activity, and it helps me think through the plan in its entirety before I begin. Does

My Childhood: Getting Over it

this limit the universe's unfolding its wonders? I respect the process and my style of reasoning and still must shift to merge the unknown into my practice. This unknown will become part of "the process". Letting things happen as they should is a harder concept for me to incorporate into my life. And yet I am finding that when I do, the results are usually better and much less complicated than my plan. When letting go and letting it happen, observe the final results. You will be delightfully surprised.

Plans do need tweaking throughout life. If we cannot let in the unknown— we are closing out this extraordinary input. Open up your ability to absorb from others, the energy, the universe (God), nature, and so much. Our imagination cannot contain what is accessible, when we allow things to unfold without interfering.

What guides your need to fullfill your percieved wants and wishes? Are you aware of how you get to what you want? Do you try to control it? Can you let it flow to you? Can you try to be the observer of your process?

Age Eleven; Tooth Extraction

eleven

tooth extraction

dental students

holding my small body down

tooth

ripped from your gums

body shaking with trauma

yes, it knows, even when you are numb

a gaping hole

the taste of iron on your tongue

part of you missing now

will the pain start

when the novocain wears off?

where's my mom?

My Childhood: Getting Over it

I'm eleven and my molar is killing me. I tell my mother, and she makes an appointment at the Eastman Dental Dispensary. In my mind, I assume Mom will take me, but she has several young kids to care for, so she gives me an assortment of coins with directions. She tells me to take the Three Lyell bus downtown, then pick up the nineteen across the street from Neisners on Main Street. I am then to get off at the large Eastman Dental Dispensary on Main Street. "What! I can't go alone! I've never taken the bus by myself!" I shriek. My tooth pulls me back to the pain in my jaw, and I recognize I must get this tooth fixed.

I trudge down busy Lyell Avenue to the bus stop which I know is in front of a dental office. I can't go to this one because the dispensary provides young dental students the opportunity to practice dentistry, and this service costs little or no money. I board the bus and vigilantly search for Neisser's at every stop on Main Street. When I spot it, I pull the buzzer wire that runs along the top of the windows on the bus. I saw other passengers exiting, pull this wire to let the driver know they wanted to get off the bus. The bus driver gives me the location of the nineteen that will continue to the dispensary. Somehow I arrive but am late, so I have to stick around until there is another available student.

Finally, after what seems like hours, I get in the chair and the dentist numbs up my jaw with Novocain. The doctor struggles to pull the tooth, and he keeps lifting my body off the chair as he pulls. He calls over several doctors to hold down my slight frame while he yanks my tooth out. It is a fucked-up experience for my eleven-year-old self. The ordeal leaves me with no outlet to express it. Angry for having to get this done alone and at the physician's roughness. Numb and packed with gauze, I leave the dispensary to navigate my way home. I am experiencing a feeling of being cut off from my body. It's tough to interpret, this sense of not feeling what just took place and still being

Age Eleven; Tooth Extraction

able to walk and think about getting home. As if I am walking next to myself and not in it.

Stopping downtown to transfer back to the three Lyell bus, I notice an ice cream truck. I run over and count my change. I have enough for an ice cream and fare to make it home. My anger justifies spending all the money that Mom gave me. She shouldn't have sent me by myself, so she will pay for my ice cream treat. So there! I prop my head against the window, riding home, while the bus rattles my skull as I lick the ice cream with a numb jaw and a sense of victory and accomplishment when familiar landmarks start to appear. When Mom asks for the change, I tell her there isn't any. She grins. Is it the dried cream mustache on my numb face?

That ride by myself was frightening. I remember thinking If I got lost, I wouldn't know how to get home. I was unfamiliar with downtown, the bus routes, and the traffic. The dispensary was an old, brick building on Main Street, with marble floors and hundreds of rooms. The large entryway echoed with noise as people passed through it. This incident gave me a recognizable feeling that would return during my childhood of being detached from the experience. The feeling of not being in my body, as if my mind put a barrier between my body and my brain. I had a traumatic tooth extraction in my fifties that bought back the same feeling when I left the dentist's office. That disconnect.

This protective action of the brain helps us get through trauma. I can now pay attention to this feeling and know I have to process and release the pain experienced. The safeguard is only a stopgap measure for survival. To thrive, that fracture must heal, both physically and emotionally. What happened, what it triggered for me, and how can I feel it and transform it into healing and growth?

My Childhood: Getting Over it

We now know that the third option one feels during trauma besides fight or flight is freeze. Much of our trauma is stored in the body in this frozen state. Getting to the frozen spots is what begins to release and heal the injury. Reenacting, talking about it, writing about it all start to unfreeze the body, and the trauma stored in your body. Have you ever felt frozen after a traumatic experience? Give it the opportunity to unfreeze. Feel it, tell it and even write about it.

Age Eleven; Church Tent Revival

Revival

always a white tent

Filled with the holy ghost

Singing, dancing, yelling

Speaking in tongues

recognizing not a word

People falling over

Amens join airborne Hallelujahs

Pentecostal religiousness

At its imaginable best

Sweat, heat, energy

Swirling, catching, trapping

Until, until you give in

Or flee

My Childhood: Getting Over it

Each year the church parishioners our family attends a Pentecostal revival meeting at a Christian camp. It is one of the significant events for the church members and a treat for kids. The encampment, an hour outside Rochester, New York, provides an exodus from the city to explore the cool park-like grounds. I have not attended the week-long camp yet. Next year I will be old enough. The compound has a little bookstore that sells bibles, books, and religious trinkets. I love this crowded, overstocked shop with more than the eyes can take in, items stacked, hanging, and sitting on the floor. A compact building across the path offers burgers and fries out of a window. The fries are crinkle-cut, served in a checkered, square cardboard container and eaten with a two-pronged wooden fork. Mom mostly packs a meal or we eat before we leave home. The occasional French fry treat imbeds its memory: hot, crispy on the outside, and chewy on the inside dipped into a touch of sweet catsup. The texture and taste combining between teeth and tongue.

The grand central superstructure houses the dormitories for the weekly camp on the second floor. A fellowship hall with an impressive kitchen is on the first. The buildings are all painted white, each of them with a wood screen door that slams shut with each entry and exit. Trails of dirt paths run from building to building. The church on the property cannot contain the revival-sized crowd. An enormous tent is setup next to the sanctuary. In the center of the compound stands a colossal tower with a considerable bell at the top, rung to announce all meals and services.

On the shores of Lake Ontario, impressive mature trees shield the sky, and green grass grows around every building, tree, and bench. For children, it is a park, a camp, and everything is open for discovery. Spending time so close to the Great Lake Ontario is a thrill for us city kids. We are free to run and play until the bell calls us to join the

Age Eleven; Church Tent Revival

mass migrating flock heading toward the large, white pavilion. We find our parents in the crowd. They are searching for their seats to hear the sermon; we hope they select seats in the back where the tent flaps are open to a breeze. The heat is stifling, suffocating the attendees during the preaching. The seating is tight in order to cram as many people inside as possible. Massive fans circulate the warm air throughout, blowing and rearranging the carefully coiffed hairdos and toupees. Up front and center is the pulpit where the preachers, singers, and announcers sit looking downward at their attendees.

Mom and Dad choose seats close to the platform so they can understand the sermon better. Ugh! The children must assemble in front of them. No giggling, pushing, pinching, or outrageous singing is tolerated by Dad. You will take a knuckle to the skull from him, called a kuponbango seven-five (pronounced coupon bango). This little nickname originates from my brother for the sound it makes on your head. He adds the seven-five for rhythm when teasing someone with his mini jingle after they receive the knuckle rap. It is fun to watch the ladies fanning, men falling asleep, the young singles making eyes at each other, the old ladies with their rolled-down stockings, and the admonishing grandmothers shaking their fingers at you. The singing, clapping, jumping, and dancing in the spirit fascinates me. I observe so much during the collection plate circulation: who donates, who pretends to give, who just passes the plate. Mom gives something, she always gives, though I do not see the denominations in her rolled-up offering.

After the preliminary monetary sacrifices and song service, the preachers get to the serious preaching at hand. Revival services outshine a normal preachment in so many ways. Preachers must uplift and stir up the spirit, and a Pentecostal address has more

My Childhood: Getting Over it

than your average gifts to share. Amens become airborne with the "Hallelujahs!" and "Preach it, Brother!" Fans flutter faster as the gentlewomen flow and dance. The speaking in tongues and shouting gets louder, more outspoken, competitive. As people fall out in the spirit, their bodies lie disorganized all over the floor. Men give up their suit coats to cover the legs of the ladies who have abandoned their modesty for religion. People crying, screaming, shaking, talking in other languages as they lay on the grass floor. Some people never stop dancing and moving, some get crazy jumping up and down, and still some just start speaking unpronounceable, non-words, clapping their hands. The cacophony of music, singing, and shouting energizes the tent, which now appears to be swaying. There are wandering ushers and deacons who attempt to get you to the front to give yourself over to the spirit. I monitor them as they meander the tent, and I wait for the moment to part the tent flaps to escape. My parents progress out into the aisle to walk to the front for the altar call, and we make a rush for it to get outside.

It is so much cooler outside as we run away from the canvas pavilion to explore. We meet up with the other kids who escaped before us. We stumble in the dark, looking for lovers embracing. We skim rocks on the moonlit lake, exploring, laughing about all we have just witnessed, mimicking and spooking each other in the dark. The glow of the tent with the organ and accordion playing is ever present in the distance. The tepee tabernacle holds all the adults inside as we continue to play recklessly. We know we must reunite with our parents to avoid a whack on the head or worse. We keep a watchful eye and ear toward the eventual exit of the saved, washed-clean, revived believers.

Age Eleven; Church Tent Revival

There were many rules and beliefs to follow in the Pentecostal theology. Words that made me shut down. "Wives be submissive to your husbands, "spare the rod and spoil the child," etc. It took me until the age of twenty-eight to leave the church, and I continued to type the monthly bulletins well after that. I remained a Sunday school teacher for several years. Breaking away from my parent's religion was one of the hardest things I did in life, leaving the only faith I knew, the one my entire family attended and continues to attend. Religion helped shape much of my childhood ethics, teaching me love for everyone "Red and yellow, black and white, Jesus loves the little children of the World." It gave me the conviction to question and not accept other's expressions of prejudice and meanness. It also broke me open with a betrayal that changed who I was for years to come. I have learned that nothing is a coincidence and my life happened exactly as it should. I am sitting here writing about my childhood because it developed precisely right. It is up to me to choose how to expand from it and reframe it.

My entire religious experience has taught me that love encompasses the endless experiences of being human. I can take what I require and drop the rest. Everyone in the building, community, belief system is subject to being imperfect. People choose their religions to match their personalities, addictions, needs, perceptions, and history. As a child, I didn't have a vote in picking my religion, but as an adult, I get to embrace what serves me best and resonates within me.

That is the beauty of choice. You do not have to follow tradition, family religions, limited to what you know. The exploration is all up to you. What do you need to experience in your faith? What is lacking or wanting from your current church? Living your authentic life includes your spiritual health. Explore, question, and embrace what you know to be true.

Age Eleven; Messin' Kids

kids messin with each other?

picking on the slighter

Running, catching

bullying

Fighting

One or the other winning

Only for the day

And then

A rerun

My Childhood: Getting Over it

Whenever Mom needs something for a recipe, she sends us to the Star Market. A few of us walk down Lyell Avenue, wait for the light at Child Street, and arrive at the grocery store with no incident. Every so often we run into a group of youngsters our age coming toward us, they stop to instigate a fight. Pushing and shoving occurs, when my brother pushes back hard, we are allowed to pass. These children become nicknamed the "messin' kids".

These scuffles escalate over time, and they are invariably on my mind if I must make the trip alone, being on alert and searching up and down the street to spot them in the distance. When I encounter them, I stand as tall as I can and look as mean as possible, they mumble remarks at me as I pass but never attempt to push me. When Mom asks me to go to the supermarket, my first thought is Will I run into the messin' kids? Upon my return, I report back to the rest of my siblings that they are looking for my brother, the one that always pushes back hard.

Other times they are in the store and follow us from aisle to aisle, saying how they will kick our asses when we get outside. Sometimes we fly all the way home, and at other points we confront them. That run feels like a race for your life as we look back to see how close they are and we reach a certain point in the race where they back off. I guess as children their rules and boundaries are still defined. We are home free once we cross Child Street. Not being one to accost and fight, I look for distractions to avoid the wrangle. Our run-in wins go back and forth depending on the group size. Frequently just a push and shove and on other occasions a bloody lip or a shiner for my brothers. My one brother seems to run into them and lose more often than not and returns with his older brother in search of the boys to seek revenge. The threat always hangs there on that slight stretch of

Age Eleven; Messin' Kids

Lyell Avenue.

We never got to learn their names and never gave ours. I wonder what their nickname for our gang was. I reminisce about those children from time to time and our altercations. Child gangs motivated by bullying. I recognize the "black sheep" in the family. The ones that my dad singles out and encourages his kids to do the same. Jokes directed toward them, as are the beatings and shaming. The bullying on another level, adult to child. As a child my empathy stays loyal to self "thank God it's not me he's berating."

I can identify the positions my siblings and I played. There are only four: The Hero, The Mascot, The Lost Child, and The Scapegoat. Each of us sometimes playing dual roles as ages and shifts in the family change. Learning how these roles still play out and the emotions behind them has helped me understand why my siblings react as they do even as adults. I know what my role represents, the positive and the negative effects of my reactions to life because of my assigned, taught role in the family. When my feelings of anger come up, I look to my role in the relationship to give me clarity in what is being triggered in me to address the fear behind that fury. What am I feeling, lacking, or wanting in the relationship? These emotions will continue to arise. My awareness is the key to dealing with them. The four family roles are:

The Hero: *The Achiever, responsible for bringing worth to the family, also a little mother or father. Parents confide in him/her. You must give up your childhood. As adults, they can have the tendency toward being a Martyr and need to control.*

My Childhood: Getting Over it

The Scapegoat: *He/she takes the pressure off the family to look no further for faults. He/she acts out unresolved issues. Black sheep, they sacrifice themselves for the family. As adults, they can feel like they don't belong, they can be self-destructive, they can take on addictions to cope.*

The Mascot: *The Clown, entertainer, they need protection, the family will hide unpleasantries from them. As adults, their lives can be chaotic, they can spiral out of control, and can develop mental illnesses.*

The Lost Child: *The family believes this child needs just to be good, they need nothing, there is no energy left for them, they must be nice. The family message is: take care of yourself. They tend to be loners, readers. As adults, they can feel empty inside and can learn not to relate; As adults they can develop patterns of depending on others instead of themselves.*

Can you identify your role from the list? How did it start? How do you interact with your parents, siblings in your role? Do you have multiiple roles? Now that you are aware do you want to change that role?

Age Eleven; Children Discipling Children

Children

Disciplining

Unconsciously hurt

Breaking others through discipline

Learning

My Childhood: Getting Over it

Children learn what they see, and discipline is no exception. My parents leave us alone with each other, usually with the eldest in charge. Devious punishment methods are invented and executed by the sibling boss.

One of the worst occurs when we do something wrong or quarrel with one another. I have to hold out my hand with the palms facing upward. The sibling in control takes a wooden spoon and doles out the preestablished punishment with the number of whacks on the palm. Reflexes don't cooperate and I lose the battle to remain still, yanking my hand back from the wooden spoon's advance, and getting only the tips of my fingers wacked. Ouch! Expecting two or more wallops gives me an unruly hand, and a do-over is ordered after each miss.

Brothers love to tease, and one time my brother gets into my little girl purse and plunders a saved dime. As I stand on the front porch, he whoops it up holding the coin, squealing, "I'm going to buy cupcakes!" before I think I yell out, "You motherfucker!" My parents aren't home, and the disciplinarian hears my God-awful statement. I blame it on my brother, but he is already off and running, leaving me standing there alone.

The punishment for swearing is given out and everyone must help. I am instructed to lie down on my belly on the sofa. The younger kids sit on my legs with one on my shoulders so I can't squirm out of the whipping. The electrical cord sears my back with each strike, stinging until it unites with the next lash, merging into a severe, painful burn. I can›t move, my back is on fire and i am thinking about the pain in my body and trying to work throough it in my brain. This is pain.

Age Eleven; Children DisciplingChildren

The siblings on top struggle to get out of the way while upholding their duties. They do not want to end up in my position.

I do not report my sister to my parents, knowing they will leave us in her care again and I will receive an even harsher punishment the next time. I cringe and feel I am already on her "bad list". I vow to never swear again and try to behave, at least while she is around.

That lashing lasts in my remembrance, and the barbarity of it haunts me. I ask, "How could she?" and I recognize the answer to my question. Children discipling children, only doing what they have experienced themselves. I too am guilty of carrying out discipline that went too far on my siblings as a child left in charge. Years later, I am reminded of an incident by a younger sibling, humbling me and letting me identify how it was possible. We learn and imitate what we are exposed to.

How much of these learned techniques did I carry into my family? I vowed to never be like my parents in discipline. However, I realize that ideas and patterns are imbedded in my subconscious, and I realize that I have subjected my children to emotional abuse. I recognize I have damaged their souls and left scars that they now carry into their families. I see it as a grandmother, and weep knowing that I taught my boys, I showed them how to behave that way. It can hurt and, yes, I agreed with my sons' souls before they were born to play the role they requested, and I am also human. It helps to understand and disconnect from both of my sons' journeys, understanding they must experience and learn from all that arrives on their own path of growth, including me.

My Childhood: Getting Over it

The wise Maya Angelo said; "When you know better, you do better." Yes, that is also true, and I know that the nature of parenthood is to give our children's souls the experiences that will allow them to heal and grow. The hardest trauma and pains are the ones that will be the biggest learning experiences. Take a look back at some of your most painful experiences. What teaching were you able to take from those experiences? Did you meet someone during that time who changed your life?

I have talked to other parents and my spouse about watching the suffering and journey of our loved ones. I appreciate that each of us cannot take the pain away from our experiences. We can commit to being there for them and allow their healing to show up, however it does. Who are we to interfere in another's life pilgrimage and mending? Do we delay the growth when we intervene in their pattern, anger, shame, or the burden they are carrying and will it be repeated until they become conscious and decide to change the direction, pattern, worthiness in their lives?

Age Twelve; Desegregation by Busing

Desegregation

Caught in the middle,

between

government

uniformed parents

who to turn to

teachers distracted

fights, slurs, hatred, anger

disorderly classrooms

desegregation

caught in the middle

between

safety

and education

My Childhood: Getting Over it

Going into the seventh grade is stressful for me. I am leaving my brothers and sisters in elementary school, riding a school bus for the first time and attending Wilson Junior High School without my older sister nearby. I am told I will catch the bus at the corner and ride to the other side of town; we will move from classroom to classroom for subjects. I am having a hard time envisioning that. This is my new routine; it is not a choice. No one explains that I have to take a bus across town because of desegregation and forced busing. My parents are not aware or don't understand what busing means. My mother receives a letter stating the school I will attend, where I will catch the bus, and what time I have to be at the designated stop. Her obligation is to get me there on time, daily.

Mom sends me to the corner on time, and I wait with several other kids and a few parents. I sit with and make friends with a small dark-haired Spanish girl named Minerva. She is beautiful, shy and scared, just like me. When the bus arrives at school, it lines up behind several buses ahead of us. We wait until it is our turn to unload. When the doors open, a gauntlet is formed by the teachers for us to walk through to the entrance. People are shouting. Police are trying to control them, and behind us a bus with children in it has a group of parents around it attempting to overturn it. The confusion, violence, and hatred on people's faces is shocking. Overwhelmed and afraid, I wonder if every day will be like this. As I transfer from one class to another during the day, fights break out in the hallways. Junior high is terrifying.

I try to explain my dread and horror to my mother, and she cannot fathom my anxiety; she tells me that's my school now. My mother does not grasp what desegregation and racial tension are or

Age Twelve; Desegregation by Busing

how to fix my problem or if it even exists. Perhaps she thinks I am exaggerating. I realize I have no out in the matter and have to deal with it myself. As the weeks progress, the riot of people lessens, and the gauntlet disappears. The fights in the corridors became fewer. However, the tension is palpable. Gym class is the worst for me, as black girls run around the locker room and pull my towel off after swimming class and laugh. When I open my locker to get dressed, they grab my expensive spray deodorant and pass it around before throwing it back at me. I am a small, shy, white, blonde girl. I cope by skipping gym class or wait in the lavatory until the locker area is empty before quickly getting dressed for my next class. I am always on alert at school now, feeling tension, observing other students and how close they get to me. I am aware of escape routes near me in case things get out of hand and a fight breaks out.

Integration entered my world because of a law passed by the U.S. Supreme Court that forced the school district to comply with busing children into different districts. The adventure made me feel unsafe, and I experienced terror in a place I should have felt protected.

Seeing and feeling the prejudice toward another race was new to me, and so was experiencing violence in school. Until integration, school had always been a safe space. The energy of the incidents is what I absorbed and felt, while unloading from the buses and all during changing classes. On the alert, to what might happen, not knowing why the black girls intimidated me and why they wanted me to fear them. I now know my soul took it all in. Neither the body or mind waits for you to understand, it goes with the feelings of the energy you are taking in.

My Childhood: Getting Over it

Growing from this experience takes many years, with other high school situations, combined with riding a public bus that puts me into similar positions. Black girls as a group would surround me and threaten to cut off my flowing blond hair, accusing me of thinking I was better than they were. I understood their anger at white people and saw and heard the racist comments directed at them in school and out. I felt their anger and saw how much they wanted to lash out at someone of the other race. I just didn't want to be the person taking the attack. TThe depth of social racism was not in my consciousness at that age. My life experiences and exposure limited to the small mostly white elementary school, my german, Italian neighborhood and my 98 percent white pentecostal church. We did have one black family in the church, the Browns and my exposure to them was wonderful. They family worshiped with us, sang with us, and were truely gracious and friendly. The only difference I recognized was the color of their skin, which was beuatiful to me. They were expressing a desire to hurt someone to mend their own hurt and I felt fear and always walked or ran away from these altercations. My fear was that they would injure me because of their own anger. Now I appreciate that the fury had nothing to do with me, and I also took my fear in until I learned to release it from my body. Becoming conscious of it when it arises starts the healing. Consciousness allows you to begin to feel and speak about those fears. You can't release or "get over it" until you allow yourself to feel what you are still "not over".

All that fear manifested into rage. The years of hatred are no longer specific to one incident in memory. It is cumulative over years of injustice, unfairness, bullying, racism, and more. The words "I'm over it now" are not enough. Mentally you think you are over it. Have you allowed your body to release and change your spirit and consciousness? Saying you're over it does not cure. Facing and feeling it moves you through it. You can't release until you own it. You can't put it down until you pick it up.

Age Twelve; Getting Evicted

Crashing down

deep

into poverty

an eviction notice

yielding the family home

accessing a rental

loss of security

trust, resources

food deprivation

Mom collapsing

into mental oblivion

is this

the definition

of hopelessness

I am twelve

and I am aware

My Childhood: Getting Over it

My mother recently brought home the last child she will give birth. She was now getting back into the rhythm of running her household. Someone knocks on the door and Mom goes to answer, finding a man with papers. His voice spreads to all of us and the little ones gather around the hem of mom's dress. We want to see and hear, in case mom needs an interpreter, but mostly because we are nosy. The guy hands my mother paperwork and tells her these are eviction orders and that we have thirty days to vacate. Dad is missing now for a few weeks, and no one knows where he is or how to contact him.

Mom calls the minister's wife, crying, and cannot figure out how or why she must give up the home she knows is hers. She doesn't understand because the mortgage is up to date. Despair is what she feels in letting go of the years of remodeling spent redoing every room. After many phone calls and a visit from the pastor's spouse, the story emerges. Dad sold our house to the dairy behind us and, yes, we must move out in a few short weeks. Ten children, a missing husband, a household full of furniture, and only a few weeks to find a new home to accommodate all. Boxes for packing, decisions about what to leave, to take. Perhaps in addition postpartum depression as she sits and cries for hours

That's when Dad arrives. I feel positive; everything will be all right now and he will end this nightmare. He takes my mother to the doctor's office to see if medicine can fix her crying because she must run a household and manage ten children. My father doesn't tell the doctor why her symptoms started. The physician hospitalizes Mom because of her nervous breakdown. I do not recollect if they hospitalized her before or after the move to Averill Avenue. I don't remember ever moving before, and this is the only house I recall living in. In hushed voices, they say he lost everything, including the car in a card

Age Twelve; Getting Evicted

game in Canada. How do you lose a house in a game of cards? Knowing how to play rummy, I can't imagine such a significant loss by playing a game. The pastor's wife looks for a place with a social worker. What can a mother with ten children do when her husband has deserted her? The women secure a rental off South Avenue across town, and we move.

The day we receive the eviction notice creates a downward spiral of disorder, fear, insecurity, and hopelessness in my tender teen years. Everything I know to be true and secure in my life breaks apart, including my parents. My dad's presence, critical to my sense of security, is gone. The days following the move are utter chaos and trauma.

We arrive at the new house and are unloading the moving truck; my brothers are sliding across the hardwood floors on the sofa cushions. They slide into one of the large dresser mirrors leaning against the wall; it crashes to the floor, cutting my brother's arm so deep he receives stitches. I see the gash and feel a heavy, ugly feeling inside me about this unfamiliar home.

The spirit of the dwelling remains foul, and many ugly events take place in the brief time we live there. I am glad to find out that shortly after we move out, they demolish the house, taking away the domain that the energy that squatted there with our misery used.

The definition of change: to become different, altered. The definition of loss is the state of being deprived of or having lost something. This story left me feeling defeated. The security in the only home I remembered and the undoing of

My Childhood: Getting Over it

our family life as I knew it. I also know that this catastrophe represented a shift in my way of living and believing. I learned that I could survive the most devastating of losses and weather change.

I had to embrace transition from a young age, continuously learning to adapt. No choices, keep pushing through and adjusting to the changes. Innovation entered my life, and I embraced it, prioritizing and thinking on my feet, correcting, accommodating, and readjusting. As a result, I don't get knocked down too easily by crisis and misadventures because I have the confidence to figure it out and move forward.

We have all heard the expression "When one door closes, another one opens." Yet we still sense fear creeping in when the door closes. Today I know that the energy and thoughts I put behind that anxiety must be positive and encouraging in order to open the next door. Trusting that it will open is not enough to get it to swing wide—you must experience how it will feel when you get what you are seeking. To feel how it will feel on the other side of the door. Feel it before you have it, give your energy the power to manifest it. Fear will always try to persuade you otherwise and definitely not want you to feel what you want. You are stronger than your greatest fear and must feel that strength in order to possess it.

Age Twelve; The R-Wing

Mental illness,

depression,

touching the brain

the body,

and the soul

locked in

my head,

a facility

unable to break out

medication blurring reality

I am no longer me

and am…….

relinquishing the quagmire of life

can I altogether let go

absolutely let go?

I'll never make it back

My Childhood: Getting Over it

We need to call someone, where's Dad. We call the preacher's wife to glance over the eviction paperwork. We learn that the papers are legal, and we have to find a place to live. Dad hasn't been around for weeks.

When Dad returns, he takes mom to the doctor's office because she cries even harder and won't talk. She is admitted to the R-Wing (psyche ward) at the hospital. After a time, Dad decides we should all go to visit Mom after church one Sunday. I remember walking down the longest winding green walled corridors to the R-Wing. These halls go on forever and the offices and waiting areas in between are more spaced apart the further we walk. This section of the Hospital feels isolated, quiet and spooky. Was my mom living here? The end of the hall deposits us in front of a thick security door with a guard. We stand between two doors, the windows around us have wires running through them. We are buzzed into the second entry door and the heavy steel door slams behind us. We are locked in.

Once inside, I see a large open make-believe living room with several couches and chairs. Glassy eyed people are sitting around watching TV in their hospital gown, slippers and some with pajamas on, hair uncombed. I wonder why they are in their pajamas in the afternoon. We wait for our mother here amongst the wild eyed and

Age Twelve; The R-Wing

dazed patients not knowing what to expect from them or our mother coming out to see us. They usher her into the room and help her sit down in a chair. We cover her with hugs and kisses and she stares straight ahead with her arms limply hanging at her side. What's wrong with my mom? Where is she? Will she always be like this? Mom, talk to us!! She is hollow, unresponsive, I feel a loss deep inside me again. I must figure this out, how can I save mom? When is she coming home? The queries run through my mind continuously. My dad's answers to my questions are shhh, talk to your mother. My mother has no response, I desperately look for that twinkle in her eye, a half-smile on her lips, something with a connection to her old self. When we leave, I peer back toward my mother to look to see if she is watching her children leave, and she continues to stare straight ahead. My stomach turns and I have a sense that my Mom is getting abused and hurt in this Psyche ward. She is medicated so greatly that she no longer exists as herself.

I do not have the capacity or wherewithal to help or protect her. I don't know what bus to catch to get me to the hospital to see her again. When is she coming home? Will she get better? I am too young to be in any adult conversations to gain answers to these questions. So, I worry and wait until I hear snippets of talk that hold a release date. The excitement is alive with the anticipation of getting back into our routine.

My Childhood: Getting Over it

Normal never returns. Mom is always forgetful and sits for hours staring off into space. She is afraid to throw anything out for fear she will lose everything again. Even spoiled milk must stay, pieces of receipts, snippets of string all valuable now. A lot of her memory is lost as we quiz her on original stories of our life. We watch in astonishment as she shakes her head and says, "I don't remember that."

The memories of mom's hospitalization gave me patience and acceptance for her, having seen the place her mind and body went to the scary institution she came back from. I also carry around resentment for years having to take care of her, watching out for her and making sure she was ok. This irritation showed up in my life as stifled anger and impatience with her. She recognized it before I did every time and I learned to see it in her reactions, then shaming myself for showing those feelings. Once I realize the pattern we had set up, I began to work on it, understanding it, and then changing it. Adjusting my responsibility took time, healing, delegating and teaching my mom. I was never completely free from the task and created peace with my mother and myself regarding our expectations of each other.

A mother and daughters' relationship is complicated enough without extraordinary circumstances. How angry do I allow myself to get with my mother? Will my exhaustive anger hurt her mental state even more? I ponder these

Age Twelve; The R-Wing

questions and approaches that will allow me to speak my feelings without crushing hers. A delicate balance of anger, acceptance, forgiveness, and shared love.

Working on responsibility for yourself is substantial work. Have you ever asked yourself what your obligation is in your relationships, yes, all of them? Is your loyalty to yourself first? Does religion dictate your parents, children, your boss, the beliefs you grew up with and were trained on? Have you evaluated your past relationships, the ones you broke away from? Did your needs come first? All significant questions that take courage to confront and make changes in order to be your best self. What responsibilities and relationships are you willing to look at today?

Age Twelve; Shoe Shining

Twelve

exposed to the world

washed-out lives

sitting

drinking

in darkness

pedophiles

attempting to extract

an opportunity

generosity

unexpected

the sleazy side of town

vacant streets

businesses closed at night

chased by shadows

driven by need

wary of entering

then going in anyway

My Childhood: Getting Over it

When you're poor, you consider ways to get cash. Steal it, earn it, haggle or scam for it. A child has little to barter. My brothers and I find means to earn it. We have one snow shovel, which requires the rest of us to steal another off a porch from the next street over to generate money. Raking leaves in the fall and shining shoes during the summer months. For shoe shining we need: several shoe polish colors, rags, water bottles, brushes, and a carrying container. We collect them any way we can.

Once gained, we can create cash. We go from bars to beer joints along the larger avenues in our territory. We then take a bus downtown to expand our turf and revenue. Each bar produces at least one customer, even if the boozer wears broken, tattered shoes. He encourages our money-making venture. I get inappropriate remarks, jokes, and requests depending on the degree of drunkenness. For me, a spit shine is always a front runner. My brother tells the customers, "We don't give those types of shines," and he says, "We have water." I don't think he understood why men would ask an adolescent girl to spit on their shoes, but he didn't like it and put a stop to it.

On a sunny afternoon we leave our first bar and start up the street; a patron follows us outside and yells out. He wants me to take off with him to his house so I can bake cookies for his wheelchair-bound mother. My brother puts himself between me and the man and says, "She's not going anywhere with you." I protest and say, "I don't mind leaving to bake cookies." My brother grabs my arm and takes a few steps forward and tells me, "He's not interested in your cookie baking skills. Now let's go." I badger him about what it was the man wanted until he says, "The man's a perv."

Age Twelve; Shoe Shining

This man's energy of deceit confuses and disgusts me; that someone wants to see me naked (that's how I translate it) is unimaginable to me.

The question, what, how people conceive these ideas toward children passes through my consciousness and then it disappears. We are on to the next establishment.

My brother recognizes my naivety and protects me, and I love him for that. Our eyes are open to other parts of humanity when we expose ourselves to the worst parts of the city and the inhabitants who turn up to greet us. However, this awareness is only as complex as our maturity.

We exposed ourselves to the ugly places that we should never have had to at a young age. The need to meet the most basic survival needs of a child makes me witness people and events that add to my existing lack of trust. The smell of a bar sticks with me through the heart when I smell it and brings back memories of adult remarks made to children and the sadness surrounding those individuals. The darkness of each place we visited obscure the other smells, smells that would be visible with light. The worn-out furniture and individuals. Hiding the uglier part of that existence in society. Shadiness inhabits the street; the daytime bustle missing, now lonely, deserted, and dark, with unfamiliar shadows. Never passing a smiling face, hurrying to the next beer joint, crossing an occasional stranger without looking up.

My Childhood: Getting Over it

During these shoe shining episodes, I observed and felt so many feelings running through my brain and body each night. Compassion, fear of safety, gratitude, humor, life. Seeing alcoholics in the bars with their unshaven faces and grubby clothes lighting up when we showed up, providing a diversion of hope. Or reminding them of their own childhood hustle. Sometimes encountering the pedophile sitting up on his stool to take notice, trying to find the weak link, ready to grab a shot at their own desperation.

Walking down abandoned streets to get to the next joint, never knowing what was lurking between the buildings in the alleys, as the sun slowly abandoned the day behind the taller buildings.

I can reflect on what I took into myself of the tattered people and their struggles. I learned that a spark always survived in that person, awakening to entertainment from innocence even if just for a few minutes. Sensing energy around me and becoming heightened and honed. I became so in tune to the spirit of strangers coming toward me who threatened my safety. That quick up-and-down look at my body, the scanning of others to see if they were paying attention. The subtle shift in a voice turning sweeter, kinder, gentler, but really not felt. Everything happens for a reason, and I learned lessons about life during our shoe shining excursions that helped me recognize and be wary. It also gave me a deep awareness of life, humanity, frailties and connections.

Sometimes it's hard to get past an incident, to draw the takeaway. I encourage every reader to pick one of those experiences in your history and ask what the takeaway was. How did it help shape the good and the terrible ideas in your life? The journey will not always be an easy one. Examining always helps you learn more about yourself. Are there smells that annoy you, soothe you or quicken something in you? Why?

Age Twelve; Children Shoplifting

hungry

team shoplifting

selecting choice items

easy to conceal and run with

children

My Childhood: Getting Over it

I address my little posse of brothers and sister, "Okay, guys, we have to put a plan together, we can't just pick up whatever we want."

"Soooo, what's on the agenda?" My brother backs me up skeptically courageous.

"Well," I say, "it has to be a meal, that's easy to hide and be enough for everyone."

"Are we going to jail if they catch us," Another asks?

"No," I respond, "we're kids, stupid, and besides, if you think you are about to get caught, run out of the fucking store as fast as you can. We'll meet at the coffee shop at the corner of Averill and South after you have your item."

Now back to the plan. Okay, there's five of us. One brother says, "I'll pick up the cans of deviled ham and a small box of Lipton tea."

Another speaks up. "That means I have to snatch the bread. That's not fair. Why do I always get the big stuff? It's harder to hide. Deviled cans of ham are small. I can put six of those in my pockets and no one will see them."

I yell, "Quit complaining, and just do it," even though he always has the harder stuff to steal because I know he is the most daring and the fastest runner.

"I'll take a box of Hamburger Helper and sugar for the tea." I instruct my brother, "You, grab the hamburg."

He complains, "What, how am I going to steal a package of meat out of the supermarket?"

Age Twelve; Children Shoplifting

"Well, shit," I answer. "My stuff is just as big, stash it under your coat."

He continues, "Yeah, but the meat is in the back of the supermarket, and there's always someone behind the meat section. It's not in an aisle where you're able to hide."

"Shut up already!" I yell. I then tell him, "You swipe a canister of a baby formula for Mike. Just take the smallest can they have. Okay, let's remember where we're meeting."

We enter the store at different times as planned. I try not to look at my siblings as I pass them in the aisles. I'm on my own mission. I know it's a sin to steal, but we do not have food or an adult at home.

I exit the store with my item and walk toward Averill Avenue without looking back, and I'm considering, hmmm . . . I'm not too sure I told the truth of not getting arrested if we are caught stealing.

When we meet up, we are short the hamburg. "You chickened out!" I bellow. "Shit! We'll have to eat the hamburger helper without the ground beef." We have a squished loaf of white bread, cans of deviled ham, formula for the baby. In the past we have given him whole milk that he puked up. We have learned that we must feed him formula. A box of hamburger helper and we'll top it off with tea. Okay, we have dinner for tonight, but we have to do this again tomorrow. I'm hoping the choices will be easier. I must think on it. Fuck! How long do we have to keep doing this?

Survival was a recurring theme in my childhood. When our core beings are under attack, and food is a basic demand of survival we can't reach for higher aspirations or ways of reasoning. I experienced this lack as a child and truly understand that when you are hungry—I don't mean when you miss a meal, I'm

My Childhood: Getting Over it

talking about not having a meal for several days—food is all that occupies your mind until you satisfy that hunger. Your worries about fitting in socially, thinking about your inner self, and belonging don't make the list until you meet that basic need first. This need even comes before safety.

Knowing you are safe goes deep when you feel it threatened as a child. I have worked hard on my right to be here. This right encompasses my entire being and how I move through life. This right gives support to my full energy being, all of my chakras. It is my right to feel, act, love, and be loved, to speak and to be heard, to see and to learn. It is the base of all the higher chakras and where I go to keep myself grounded. Your belief in this right must be strong and persuasive to support your chakras.

Where do you stand on your most basic need? How has your childhood affected this belief? Get real with the conviction that being on this planet gives you the right to be here. Every person in this world has merited the right to heal, to be loved, and to grow into who you are meant to be. Yes, every human being. Are you willing to explore your thoughts, your rights? Your chakras?

Age Twelve; Mom Walking Out

In a trance

she grabs a chair

steps up

walks across the counter

and out

through the window

in broad daylight

unaware of the four-foot drop

her pain is so harrowing

she walks away

from eight children

including her baby

never looking back

disappearing

down South Avenue

My Childhood: Getting Over it

They release my mother from the R Wing before she should have been. My dad has to serve jail time, and he insists mom has to be there to take care of us. She has been in the R Wing (mental ward at the hospital) for a few weeks after intensive shock treatments. Dad explains to the doctor that nine kids need their mother. I believe he takes her out against doctor's orders.

My mother arrives, and Dad leaves for prison. She sits on the floor for days with her legs up against her chest rocking, without speaking. I try to get her to eat and take care of my four-month-old brother so I can go back to school. She doesn't respond and stares out into space.

One day when I am trying to get through to her, she calmly stands up and pulls a chair next to the kitchen counter. She steps up and walks across the countertop as she grabs a frying pan from the sink and then smashes the kitchen window. She steps out the window like it was a doorway onto the driveway four feet below. I can't run after her because I have the baby, but I watch her walk toward South Avenue away from us, the broken glass, and her four month old baby.

When my brothers and sisters come home from school, I go looking for my mom and find her in an alley sitting behind a dumpster in that same dazed, fetal state. I bring her food later that evening and look for her every night. Some nights I find her and other nights I don't. On nights I find her she takes the food but never speaks.

The Board of Education sends a truancy officer to the house because I have missed so much time from school. He has come before, and I haven't answered the door. Today I answer, not knowing why and he discovers me at home with a preschooler and a four-month-old baby. Social Services sends an African American woman to live with us for a while, and she introduces the family to soul food and bingo.

Age Twelve; Mom Walking Out

It frees me up to attend classes again and not worry about my two youngest siblings. Our live-in homemaker lets me be myself again and also gives me someone else to focus on. She is funny, loud and so culturally different from what I know, it delights me. I wonder how long this will last. I sneak out with food after dark to look for my mother and bring her news of what's happening at home.

I recognized that day my mother left in hopelessness in an altered state, and I hoped she would return. Gone from her mind and body. She returned physically, but her mind never really came back to the mother I knew before her shock treatments. At twelve, what could I have possibly understood about what my mother was going through? I now appreciate that life can knock you down so hard it takes much to regain your normal again. I also realize that drugs and mind-altering treatments can damage to a great degree. Complete recovery doesn't always happen, and the life you get to live isn't necessarily a conscious choice.

It is not our responsibility to see or understand others' minds. We can only be present for individuals, to allow them to express themselves, be there enough to encourage or shed light on their day with our presence or words. And sometimes we ourselves cannot be present because of our own pain. I had days when all I could be was an observer of my mother's world. Her choices, her life, my choices, my life. No amount of cajoling, teasing, guiding, pretending, encouraging worked. Giving myself permission to let go removed me from living an existence of frustration in trying to have control. As an adult I was not in command of my mother's life as much as I tried to convince myself.

Be an observer more and more, detach from others' lives. Love them, don't try to control them or the relationship you are in with them.

My Childhood: Getting Over it

Ask them if they want your advice before giving it. Make it your uncommon pattern, permission, before you enter. Your appreciation for their adventure will grow exponentially. Who in your life do you feel you have to control the most, start there. Observe.

Age Twelve; Getting Mugged

walking down the middle of the street

Suddenly surrounded

they want what we have

too angry

to perceive the peril

I say

Fuck you, mother fuckers

And then a Jab to my eye

then my gut

a flash of a knife

an elderly lady from her porch

yells out

sirens in the distance

Just in time

Mugged

then

Saved

My Childhood: Getting Over it

My younger brother and I are heading out to take the bus downtown to earn some money by shining shoes. My parents are absent from our home, but the authorities don't realize it yet. Dad is in prison and Mom has left the house and is living on the streets after being released too early from the psych ward. We both have two dimes each for one-way bus fare to downtown and we stroll up several blocks to catch a bus. This trip will get my brother and I closer to the sleazier side of town where more of the beer joints are.

While walking down the middle of our narrow street, we notice a youthful gang striding toward us. We make the decision between ourselves to stand our ground and continue to strut. We find this decision turns out to be unwise, as the teens grab my skinny brother; he gives up his money. I step backward and refuse to surrender my two dimes on principle. My twelve-year-old ego knows what is right and wrong, and they are mistaken for trying to take what is mine. After a few jabs in the stomach, a black eye, and the flash of a knife, an old lady comes out on her stoop yelling, "The police are on their way!" She beckons us onto her porch. We race up to the landing while the thugs run away as we hear a siren in the distance.

I am shaking from the incident yet proud that I still have my twenty cents in my pocket. After accessing my bruises, I realize how serious the attack could have been. Was my principle worth my life? The lady tells us to wait until the boys are out of sight because she doesn't have a phone and law enforcement is not coming.

That old, gracious hero who lies so convincingly shows up as my angel that day. My brother chastises me for not giving up my dimes, which means nothing to my twelve-year-old, stubborn self. Still trembling, I feel as if I won the battle.

Age Twelve; Getting Mugged

We walk downtown after the incident, knowing we have to make money to get something to eat and then go home.

Oh, my young self, what I could teach you now, and what I know, respecting the outrage you had within yourself. Anger that puts your own safety at risk. Your anger when finally released, settles your risk-taking, giving yourself the love and value, you crave. Putting myself at risk or jeopardizing myself played out more times than I wanted. The rage inside guaranteed my subconscious into believing I was valuable enough to protect and keep safe.

Confrontation was easier when I had anger to drive it into action. As I agee the conflict takes a back seat to awareness. Awareness of what to confront. It's not the others reaction coming toward me, its my reaction rising up to see myself in the other. The mirror to my own trigger. Thank you for letting me see myself in you. Thank you.

We are all worthy, good enough, lovable, and unique, one of a kind, with our own special gifts to bring to the world. Anger shows up in so many disguises, tricking us into thinking the worst of ourselves. When it shows up, know that it is anxiety, self-doubt, that is your clue. Give it a voice. Ask why it is showing up now. Say hello to it, face it, and challenge it. Ask it what it is afraid of. Is the fear necessary, or is it a caution?

Age Thirteen; Haunted House

The House

Filled with evil

Darkness, horror, terror

Unimaginable cloaked ghosts

Haunted

My Childhood: Getting Over it

Our house on Averill Avenue is a haunted house. My mother walks through the kitchen window to live on the streets. A chunk of my brother's arm is almost cut out on the first day we move in when he crashes into a dresser mirror while sliding across the living room floor on a sofa cushion. Both of my sister's wrists are slashed when she falls into a broken pot and she almost bleeds to death. A group of no less than twenty-five kids chant for my brother in front of our home for him to come out so they can kick his ass. I get mugged after just leaving the house to go shoe shining. I stab one of my brothers with a fork while cooking Hamburger Helper because he wants to taste it. The man next door is a pedophile, always beckoning me to come into his house while his fat girlfriend smiles. My job is to lead eight kids struggling to survive without Mom or Dad by stealing food at the local grocery store. While simultaneously trying to take care of a four-month-old baby. I get my period for the first time, with no one to get guidance from and no money to buy my girl supplies with. We live there for just over a year.

The worst night is when my dad comes home from prison. Mom is back at home, and when dad arrives, they have a horrific, violent fight. My dad goes down to the cellar and unscrews the fuses in the electric box, and darkness and fear descend on the house. I hear my mother screaming. The little ones crawl under the dining room table. Objects fly and smash in the dark. I run to the nearest pay phone and call the cops and wait outside, afraid to go back in the house of terror. I follow the police into the house with their flashlights beaming all over the place, and my dad passes us in the darkness on his way out, shouting, "He's inside, get him, he's inside!"

Age Thirteen; Haunted House

The chaos of the cops, radios, voices, kids screaming, police talking to each other mutes my yelling over and over, "You're letting him get away, that's him!" By the time we get inside, Dad is long gone.

My mother asks me to turn the fuses back on in the basement, adding to my terror. The cellar stairs do not have backs on them, and my biggest fear of going into the dark, dank, moldy cellar is that someone will reach out between those steps and grab my ankles. I fly down holding a cop's flashlight and rotate the fuses, then run back up the staircase, planning to scream to the ends of the earth if that hand came out from the stairs.

My mother's children are crying, my mother is bleeding, the house is in shambles, chairs and tables overturned, with broken glass everywhere. The police promise to look for him while patrolling the neighborhood, and leave. We do not feel safe and wonder all night if he is returning. Talking among ourselves about our fears, we lock and block the doorways, knowing there are plenty of windows that he can break.

Was the house haunted, or was it my child's mind rationalizing the unbelievable terror in my life that felt like a horror thriller movie? To this day, my brothers and sisters and I agree it was the house, because so many unpleasant things happened in the brief span of time we lived there.

Again, this story is about energy and also fear. Was the spirit already there, or did we as an uprooted, fearful family generate this tremendous energy? We were children struggling with the unimaginable fear of survival. The neighborhood surrounding us was fearful and also struggling in poverty and crime.

My Childhood: Getting Over it

This energy culminated into our only explanation of a haunted house. I know the energy you give out will be the same coming back to you.

The fear of survival is the basic need in our subconscious even before we are born. I know my anxiety about survival surrounded my fears.

I am still here, enduring, knowing I can provide for myself and I have the power to set up my own protected space. My safe space, including my physical and spiritual surroundings. Our basic and first chakra is the right to be here. This chakra was the first to enter my attention for mending. I realized I was here, and so it is that I am supposed to be here. However, I got to understand what that "right" literally meant, and with that right came my obligation to cultivate and restore my belief in that idea and energy.

More than providing myself with a secure home, I had to eliminate threats, and toxic, angry people. I had to give myself a world where I didn't have to be on alert to what was coming at me psychologically, emotionally, and spiritually. Being on alert brings me back to survival. I cannot live on alert anymore and I cannot alter people. I can only change myself, my surroundings and my energy. I have that power. Everyone does. What kind of energy do you generate and allow around you? Creating a peaceful life of love is the same energy I want coming back toward me.

Age Thirteen; White Tablecloths

Pure white table cloths

Warm glowing candles, I dream

I'll sit there someday

My Childhood: Getting Over it

Thirteen, managing, and maneuvering my way home from school. We have just moved from living three blocks from the junior high school I attend to across town. The daily trek home includes taking a bus downtown and then transferring to another to get home. All the buses pass through downtown on Main Street and on to their designated routes.

I have made this trip several times now and curse the transfer prerequisite. Ten buses pull up in front of the Sibley's building and hundreds of people jam to get on-board, pushing and shoving their way to the doors. I have to board the nineteen Thurston. I walk the line to find the nineteen and push my way through to the front, ensuring an actual boarding. I learn the first time that the door closes when the bus gets full and another half-hour to forty-five-minute wait means darkness when I reach home.

It is the time of the year that doesn't guarantee warm days, and hanging outside is another fight. I huddle in a building entrance to keep out of the wind and bitter chill.

I follow the line to the end one day and don't find a nineteen in the line. As I peer past the line, I see more buses around the corner waiting for the mass to clear out before they edge up to turn the corner.

Hmm . . . I figure if I walk back two blocks I can get on before the mad mob.

Main Street intersects with three streets before the Sibley building. Which one holds my bus? A driver tells me to walk up around the corner to East Avenue to catch the nineteen.

Age Thirteen; White Tablecloths

On this dreary late fall day in Rochester, New York, the sun is behind the clouds and they are getting darker than usual as a storm is arriving. It excites me to test my newfound information.

I don't wait for the Main Street lineup. I walk up the two blocks and find the first stop on East Avenue and wait. It starts to rain wet snow, and I back away from the stop and snuggle up against the building.

As the wind picks up, I turn around and face the window. I am suddenly enchanted by the most beautiful view . . .

A restaurant with white tablecloths, each table displaying a flickering, candlelit orb. The dim lights on the tables, invite you to sit and enjoy an intimate dinner.

I am hypnotized by the view and feeling of luxury, wealth, and warmth. Such abundant extravagance is unfamiliar to me.

Before I can reflect on or process the vision, I say to my young self, "I'm going to eat in a restaurant like this one day." The sound of a bus and the smell of diesel breaks my spell as the bus arrives at the stop.

I can place myself back in that moment and experience the richness, extravagance, and warmth. I can see the tables on one side of the glass with my thirteen-year-old self on the other. Standing there in the cold, snowy rain with my hand-me-down clothes. Waiting for the bus to get home to the Section Eight public housing and my single mom with eight children. And still, somehow, my young girl self could claim with such confidence that she would dine in a restaurant like that someday. I have since dined in restaurants with white tablecloths and am always delighted by this recollection and that of my thirteen-year-old self's audacity to dream.

My Childhood: Getting Over it

"The only unreachable dream is the one you don't reach for." I love this beautiful quote by Abhishek Shukla. I still thrill myself every time I dare to fantasize and I manifest a thought. This story usually enters my mind because the sight in front of me was so surreal and unobtainable and yet . . . Dreaming changes our brains, because we are literally feeling what the possibility would feel like. The universe pulls in these vibrations to give us what we want. If you pray, your wish (prayer) goes up to your God, and your desires, needs are met by whoever you believe in, because of your vibrational energy.

I didn't always have this knowledge of the power we all have to manifest what we want in our lives. I now have the knowledge and the power to create all that I need and want. It is no longer called daydreaming, because these dreams have come true for me so many times in my life.

It is a tremendous power to have in your possession. Do you dream and feel as if that wish has already been granted? Letting it go to feel the energy of having it. Do it and it will be yours.

Age Thirteen;
Tea with No Sugar

A daily specialty

tasting for the first time

without sugar

Its natural flavor

Somewhat bitter

craving that sweetness

because of the lacking

I pay attention

to what is present

My Childhood: Getting Over it

We always have tea and sugar in the house. It is Mom's go-to drink, and we relax and usually sip it in the evening. Mom refuses to go to Westfall Road to sign up for welfare assistance, and my dad is in and out of our lives. "Westfall Rd; Monroe County Department of Human Services that This area of human services encompasses Temporary Assistance, Emergency Assistance, SNAP (Supplemental Nutrition Assistance Program), Medicaid, Home Energy Assistance Program (HEAP), Child Support Enforcement and Day Care subsidies for working parents.

It also encompasses Child Protective Services (CPS) Foster Care, Adoption, Adult Protective Services (APS), and other family services teams such as, the Youth Opportunity Unit (YOU), Family Access and Connection Team (FACT)." When Dad stays at home for any length of time, he always gets money to buy groceries. When he leaves for weeks, those groceries dwindle to absolutely nothing.

Our pantry has built-in glass cupboards on top and cabinets below. Sometimes the cupboard is positively bare—not a can or carton on the shelves. Our last box of pekoe is shrinking. We try to make money doing chores in the neighborhood and still have to resort to stealing until Dad shows up. I start a pot of brew and looked for a sweetener everywhere, because I cannot imagine drinking it without the sweetness I crave and want.

I settle for unsweetened tea and slowly sip it, tasting the bitterness. Afterwards, I lie on the couch and listen to my body. The hunger makes me so weak and tired. My mind concentrates and pays attention to how the physical pain feels. I fall asleep with those feelings.

Age Thirteen; Tea with No Sugar

The meal comes from somewhere; I don't remember if it's a church drop-off, or if my father returns with groceries.

It could have been my siblings returning from a stealing spree.

I learn that food always, always, always tastes better when you are hungry.

Do we have to lack or lose in order to enjoy? I need to take moments where I stop and just appreciate. The taste of food, the surrounding smells, the gorgeousness of a person and the depth of others' souls. I am working hard on being present in the moment, and it brings me closer to others and myself. The noise of living disappears for a bit, then grows as these smaller moments merge into one another. Loving life changes who you are. Gratitude!

When I am present sipping tea, i take in the warmth, the smell, the steam and the taste. It is easy to be present with tea. I want to be tea present in all areas of my life. Present with the sounds, the wrinkles (mine and others) the smiles, tastes, feelings, breezes blowing, birds chirping. I want to be present in life.

Have you ever noticed how much you miss someone or something once it is gone? Is that one of those happenings in life is a reminder to appreciate what you have today, every day? Oh, yeah that gratitude!!

Age Fourteen; Free Samples

Expecting an abundance

more that you can eat in one day

snacks, cookies, treats

a child's dream

opening the carton

not recognizing the bounty

oh, sorry, boys, not for you

a considerable largess for girls

My Childhood: Getting Over it

A funny incident occurs with my younger brothers involving theft when I was fourteen. Yes, theft. It is an enjoyable summer morning, with the boys looking for adventures to pass the day. A company drops off boxes filled with samples at the corner of each street. Whether it is detergent or cookies, we don't know until they make the delivery. The mail carrier's job is to open these packs and deliver one sample to each house on that street. During this summer morning bike ride, my brother spots a large parcel at the end of our street. My brothers' expectations for the samples are cookies or a snack, and a plan hatches and is ready to be carried out.

Why settle for one sample of cookies when we can get a full carton? The plan is to walk to the corner with the red wagon and bring the box to the garage, while averting Mom. I stay in the garage waiting for the surprise with anticipation. No one thinks to open the parcel before hauling it home, so not so discreetly they transfer the box. Huddling around the unveiling, I read "Kotex" on the side. I immediately identify the contents, but my brothers continue ripping with fantasies of Oreos.

The boys rip open the compact individual packages only to reveal a pad being promoted by Kotex. As they free the pad from its little container, they questioned me, "What the fuck are these"? I respond with a colossal smile and answer, "They are for when you get your period." They simultaneously drop the pads and yell "Ughhhh!" The boys wander off, disenchanted but not discouraged from their next escapade. My smile never fades as I carry the cache of boxes upstairs to share with my sisters.

Age Fourteen; Free Samples

Unexpected gifts delight no matter how old you are. This gift showed up for the girls in the family. Those pads kept us supplied for quite a while. One less worry on an adolescent's list of must-have amenities. Waiting for one thing and getting another. Neither one disappointing.

Sometimes in life we expect something and it shows up in a different way. I am always thrilled when that happens. It reminds me again to let it happen, as it will, because when it shows up, I say hmm, I would have never thought of that.

Have you ever thought that you knew exactly how a person will respond or how an event would turn out only to be surprised that the person or event was or said something better than you expected? Begin to pay attention to your thoughts and where they go when you are expecting something. Can you let go of the expectation and just allow it to arrive.

Age Fourteen; Apu Getting Off the Bus

Adjusting your mood

Watching for signs

A happy gait

A stumbling gait

A steadfast angry walk

Knowing

And then

Awaiting his arrival

I have learned

To watch

And adjust

My Childhood: Getting Over it

Because we have a collection of kids in our family, we attract more from the neighborhood. We never lack enough players for baseball, tag, chiller, or just hanging out. We hang out on the beautiful majestic trees lining Penhurst St on both sides shading us from the hot summer sun. We get very little traffice on the stree. We hold tennis tournaments with nets and boundaries chalked out on the street pavement. Future players watch intensely as they relax on the grass between the sidewalk and the blacktop. Arguments and settlements rise and fall as the hours of summer pass. We make up rules regarding the curb. We change kickball and whiffle baseball rules to accommodate our hard-surface playground. The screams of joy and anger fill the air, annoying the older neighbors. We have our roles: leader, followers, jokers, and, of course, the instigators. But what fun we have never getting too hot under the umbrella of the tallest mature trees that protect us from burning. We forget or can't break away from the game to go in and eat with the winning score at stake as we play in front of the house.

The day turns into late afternoon, our attention is drawn to the sound of the bus doors opening at the end of the street. He has to walk the distance of about fifteen houses. When we hear the CHH-HHHH of the doors, everyone stops and looks toward the corner. If Apu steps off the bus, the other kids— brothers, sisters, and friends— take off for home. The kids in the neighborhood whisper "Apu" (which means Dad in Hungarian). They know that cussing will ensue, and we run into the house out of embarrassment. Apu doesn't hesitate to cuss anyone out, it doesn't matter if you are ten or seventy-five. I always wait a few more minutes watching Apu's walk down the sidewalk before heading into the house. I can interpret his stride and tell if he is having a good or a nasty drunk and adjust.

Age Fourteen; Apu Getting Off the Bus

A good drunk means he will be silly and generous. If he has any money, and we ask for it for new shoes or clothes, he gives it. He jokes with Mom the entire night with hugs and kisses. A nasty drunk most often ends with a quarrel, some bodily violence toward Mom or some of his children, the rest of us hiding in our rooms until he falls asleep. Sometimes these arguments end up with police calls when Apu goes too far in beating my mother. My job is to ride my bike up to the bowling alley with my brother to call the cops and then step between my parents until the police arrive. If Dad goes to jail, then it is quiet for the night and we can relax and sleep peacefully. Consoling Mom and helping her clean up the blood on her face, straightening her hair, and furniture before goint to bed.

As a young teen, that sound of the bus door opening starts a reaction in me that leaves me with unpredictability and uneasiness. Scanning for clues, that signal the adjustment needed for the right mode of reaction, not what I'm feeling but how I must react. That is what happens to traumatized children. Never knowing what kind of drunk was walking through the door put me on high alert throughout my childhood. I now know that this high-alert status changed my body, my brain, and the "dis-eases" I got later in life. All of my diseases are autoimmune diseases and are directly related to chronic, unpredictable stress. These stressors trigger low-grade inflammation in the brain, creating a state of neuroinflammation which then develops a type of non-neural brain cell known as microglia, which impacts the entire body. Our brains trigger the release of hormones that course through our bodies, hormones that impact cells in our entire body. The Adverse Childhood Experiences (ACE) Survey includes ten questions about your childhood asking you simply if these ten things occurred or not, yes or no.

My Childhood: Getting Over it

If a woman answers yes to three of the ten questions the likelihood of developing an autoimmune disease later in life increases by twenty percent; for men, it is ten percent.

This study was conducted for over twenty years by the Center for Disease Control (CDC).

Working to heal these diseases is possible, and knowing how they manifested in my body gave me great relief, because it was not entirely my fault. My body reacted to the constant alert signals bombarding me physically, changing my brain neurons and genes. The cells in my body were registering my feelings, fears, and traumas, changing my cell structures, which impacted my immune system. I want everyone to know that your body also reacted to your own trauma—changing cells, adding patterns, and creating the body you now possess.

The great news is that we can heal. There are alternative healing therapies that can heal your body. Meditation, yoga, massage, breathwork, myofascial message therapy, cranial message therapy, psychodrama therapy, creative writing, painting, improvisation, and so much more. Remember to keep in mind that body movement must be involved in this work.

Age Fourteen; Apu Getting Off the Bus

Adverse Childhood Experience (ACE) Questionnaire

Finding your ACE Score

While you were growing up, during your first 18 years of life:

1. Did a parent or other adult in the household often ...Swear at you, insult you, put you down, or humiliate you? or Act in a way that made you afraid that you might be physically hurt?   Yes, No   If yes enter 1 _____

2. Did a parent or other adult in the household often ... Push, grab, slap, or throw something at you? Or. Ever hit you so hard that you had marks or were injured?   Yes, No   If yes enter 1 __

3. Did an adult or person at least 5 years older than you ever...Touch or fondle you or have you touch their body in a sexual way? or Try to or actually have oral, anal, or vaginal sex with you? Yes, No If yes enter 1__

4. Did you often feel that ...No one in your family loved you or thought you were important or special? or your family didn't look out for each other, feel close to each other, or support each other? Yes, No If yes enter 1 __

5. Did you often feel that ...You didn't have enough to eat, had to wear dirty clothes, and had no one to protect you? or Your parents were too drunk or high to take care of you or take you to the doctor if you needed it? Yes, No If yes enter 1 _____

6. Were your parents ever separated or divorced? Yes, No If yes enter 1 _____

7. Was your mother or stepmother: Often pushed, grabbed, slapped, or had something thrown at her? or
Sometimes or often kicked, bitten, hit with a fist, or hit with something hard? Or Ever repeatedly hit over at least a few minutes or threatened with a gun or knife? Yes, No If yes enter 1 __

8. Did you live with anyone who was a problem drinker or alcoholic or who used street drugs? Yes, No   If yes enter 1   _____

9. Was a household member depressed or mentally ill or did a household member attempt suicide?   Yes, No   If yes enter 1   _____

10. Did a household member go to prison? Yes, No If yes enter 1 _____

Now add up your "Yes" answers: _____ This is your ACE Score

Age Fourteen; Encyclopedias

Heavy

Before smart phones

Encyclopedias

For the year purchased and before

I learn

My Childhood: Getting Over it

Most of us are in junior or high school the day the encyclopedia salesman knocks on our door. He talks to my father, showing him several of the books with illustrations. Noticing the kids running around, he convinces my dad that his children would excel in school with this tool, as it was akin to having a library in your home. The salesmen's talking points, techniques, and presentation enthrall me. He persuades my dad that his kids should have this knowledge at their disposal and excel in academics.

The cost of these splendid volumes is not cheap, costing hundreds of dollars with options. Your options include getting the yearly updated World Book Special Addition; six-month financing, one-year financing, and the extended three-year financing. Our father negotiates until he secures the World Books for his children. He is so proud of this gift he can give to help educate his children.

When they arrive, these books lock everyone into two hours of studying per weeknight whether or not we have homework. Dad's new mantra is that we now "have a library at our disposal," and we can read volumes nightly even if our teachers don't assign work.

My brothers flip through the encyclopedias until they find an interesting anatomical picture and point it out to everyone. This sends us all into uncontrollable fits of snickering. Dad comes out to the dining room to find giggling and give the boys his famous knuckle to the Head. He reads these informative books himself and every so often he comes out to the table to educate his offspring on things he thinks are beneficial to our education.

Those encyclopedias unite the siblings at the dining table—we secretly and quietly communicate. We are always searching for pictures of abnormal diseases with accompanying pictures. The laminate pages of the body that overlay eachother are the coolest.

Age Fourteen; Encyclopedias

On one occasion Dad has the girls leave the room because he must educate the boys on serious business.

The next day we ladies try to get a moment alone with the lads to learn what this education was. Our brothers can barely get the story out without howling. They began flipping through the pages, trying to find the exact pictures of "the disease." The one with the oozing blisters and bumps on people's hands. When they finally located the illustration and we see it, they say "Dad said that this is what will happen if we masturbate." We fall to the floor laughing. The encyclopedias are priceless.

My dad always stressed learning and how important it was for us to get our education to be successful. He worked so hard to drive that into us. I thank him for that, knowing he sparked the seed in me to learn long after school and that seed has grown into such lucious and exotic greenery in my life.

Learning changes the brain and opens the mind to alternative possibilities and adventures. We grow in relation to our learning. I am referring to every kind of information, not just reading. Study expands us. I continue to grow through my education of my history, its traumas, and the healing that is so available to me through my desire to pursue it.

What do you want to learn and explore about yourself, your history, your patterns, and your relationships? Learning about yourself will amaze and awe you. Your specialness deserves acknowledgement. Explore who you are, learn who you are, your full potential and so much more. Learning is limitless.

Age Sixteen; Dislocating My Elbow

Talking, then not

pain filling the silence

an understanding between the two

don't show each other emotions

weakness

punishing with silence

a patten emerges

and thinking...

I can live with this

My Childhood: Getting Over it

At sixteen, I was the oldest member of our roving band. My brothers and I with a few friends travel the streets or walk up to Genesee Valley Park to play tennis. When my father is around, his rule is we must be back for supper. This one evening we are late and Mom has served dinner and Dad is in a mood. When his anger overtakes him, he wails on one of my brothers. I never expect him to strike me because I am his golden child. But today is different, and he blames me because I am the eldest in the group and answerable for having everyone home for dinner. Hmmm, did he suspect that I met my boyfriend during our tennis matches? We paid off my little band to go to the bodega several blocks away so we could be alone? I am at that age, turning into a young lady. Is that why he's angry, seeking me out today. Is he uncomfortable with my changing body and attitude and aware of what is out in the world waiting for me?

But before my mind could work this out, my father grabs my hair and throws me across the room, not realizing that an eighty-five-pound girl is going to fly through the air. I put my arms out to break the fall against the stairs, and when I land, I watch my right arm bend backward at the elbow, sending me into a terror as I run out of the house. My brother returns my arm to my chest and tells me to hold it upright and runs to a neighbor's home to call a taxi to bring me to the emergency room. To pay the fare, he spends the little bit of money that he has made from doing odd jobs in the neighborhood. Neither of my parents come to the hospital. My dislocated elbow is reset and a cast is applied. I don't remember talking to anyone about paying for this visit. My brother must have told the receptionist we were on Medicaid and gave them my parents' name. I know a social worker got involved at the emergency room, so she probably was able to determine or find our name in a database.

Resetting my arm is easy compared to the thought of facing

Age Sixteen; Dislocating My Elbow

my dad, which petrifies me. I understand it was an accident by the look on his face just after he threw me. Dad rarely got violent with me. Yes, he'd kick my siblings' asses, but not mine. My feelings terrify me. I love my dad. How can I communicate that I recognize he didn't mean to dislocate my elbow? I want him to get that I know it was an accident without becoming emotional by crying. If I cry, he might cry, and that just can't happen. And so, I just don't speak to him. I learn how powerful punishing with silence is. The Department of Social Services (DSS) comes to investigate and interrogate me. I let them know that dad didn't intentionally dislocate my elbow and I was not afraid of my dad. I tell them do not want to leave my home.

Dad and I understand that I elect to stay home, and by me not talking to him, we accept and reconcile our hurts, anger, and mistakes without having to discuss them with feelings. The future brings more arguments between Dad and me, always ending in muteness and then reconciling with our shared awareness of what not talking meant. Not speaking words speaks volumes when one knows the code.

I used this non-talking technique with my dad and later with my husbands and, I assumed, I was punishing them. I always considered it as torture to them until I processed this story and the silence origination. It was about not speaking about the pain, and not showing my weak side, which would lead to crying and being sorry. My dad could not show me his weak side and admit his shortcomings and anger. I could not show my tender side to him because it might activate his gentler side. The muteness was not a punishment; it was simply easier because our emotions were removed and we could move past the incident without feeling.

My Childhood: Getting Over it

I know I have practiced other patterns in which I felt I had to hide my emotions, like laughing instead of crying, ignoring, pretending I didn't hear, in order not to feel. I can now see this silence really only punished me. Yes, my husbands might feel bad, but I was withholding anger and feelings inside me during those silent periods, which sometimes lasted for a week. Oh! What a shame. If one reader can recognize their own system of silence and how it affects them from this book, I will feel I have completed my mission for its stories.

Explore your silence: what does it represent, and how did it start? What are you holding in and not speaking about or feeling? Is it really serving you? Be courageous, be vulnerable and say what you feel instead of practicing silence. It gets easier, the more you do it.

Age Sixteen; Where Are You, God?

The Almighty - written at age sixteen

This one that is omnipotent
Who can do most anything
We call his works magnificent
His miracles exalting

But when he takes a dear life
We accept it as his will
We put aside all distress and strife
He knows which ones to kill

Prayers to him are just our will
he has not time for us
He allows us to become so ill
For this he's called so gracious

Our flawless God is so full of power
The earth he destroys so fully
For this we love him ever dearer
Our reward, destruction completely

My Childhood: Getting Over it

He came in the form of a dove in a disguise to fool us all
So, we gave him freely of our love
Couldn't see the coming of our fall

He brings us all such sorrow
Our God's unlimited power
We know not what may come tomorrow
Or if we'll see another flower

When I was about sixteen years old, I became aware of how my body and thoughts were changing. At this age, I am afraid of growing up and also don't want to be a teenager anymore. When I make out with a boy, I love the physical feelings coursing through my body for the first time. My imagination running so far ahead of me, with my body yelling, "Wait up!" The few romance novels I've read have not exaggerated their description of romance, love, dizziness, and being weak in the knees.

Hanging out with my brothers and the boys in the neighborhood has taught me that the talk about loose girls is ruthless. The nicknames rhyme with cruelty. Not having experienced sex yet, I cannot imagine the event and all that comes with it. So, I am aware of a reputation even as I progress in making out. Stopping before, in order to preserve my good name at the expense of my frustrated and curious hyper sensitive body.

Being raised in the church brings with it such a conflict in morals. I voice my opinion to the pastor and his wife that the Almighty did not make something feel so good if it was so bad. I share some of my

Age Sixteen; Where Are You, God?

concerns and questions with my minister (Rev, shortened from Reverend during my rebellious adolescence), arguing, contemplating, seeking truths, and sharing. He is my second dad, whom I share everything with. He picks me and my brothers and sisters up three times a week to attend church and brings us home on each of those nights. He is the man who talks to my father when dad beats my mother up and sets my dad back on the right path. My mother trusts him with her children. She entertains him and his family after Sunday services with lavish dinners. The family adores him, and he can do no wrong. Rev is a gentle, soft-spoken guy who never loses his temper or yells. I admire his faith in God and his dedication to his parishioners.

Rev picks me up without my siblings and we are alone in the sanctuary walking toward the front of the church along the back wall. He pushes me against the wall and gropes my breasts. His hand grabs my hand and puts it on his erect penis, directing me to fondle it. He presses his body against mine, trapping me against the wall.

My initial shock is followed by outrage and disgust. I get out of his trap several times and he continues pushing me back into the corner. I struggle with freeing myself. I frantically ask what is happening, who is this man, and why is he trying to have sex with me? I try to figure out how to stop this; it is hard to break free from his strength.

The next time I break free, I run to his office, lock myself in, and threaten to call his wife if he doesn't take me home. He promises he will drive me home so I come out. I sit in the back seat as he drives me home, trying to explain what happened. He is telling me he didn't mean to go that far and how sorry he was. I have no voice to express my outrage, and I cannot take in his voice or justification.

My Childhood: Getting Over it

I attempt to process what happened but have no context with which to compare it. I am devastated by his betrayal as a father, spiritual guide, man, and leader of the community. I ask myself how all the good I know about him can be so wrong? He was in his fifties; did he think I was open to having sex with him? Was it my fault? I can't comprehend what just happened with the gentlest man I know.

During the next few weeks, he continues to grab me when no one is around. He watches when I go into his office to turn off the sound system after service; he locks the doors and corners me. I see how bold he is getting. It seemed as if he was daring someone to catch him. I live in fear of being caught with him fondling me. I stop taking care of the duties I have performed for years in the sanctuary. I hang out with my brothers and sisters outside the church, waiting for the ride home.

I question my faith in God and all he represents to me, the church, and men. Where is God, how did he allow this to happen? Will all men I love and respect be like him? If I tell, who will believe me? His betrayal would devastate my parents. My dad is already drinking beyond control. What could this knowledge do to his faith and health? My mother's faith in her religion is so strong and is one of the good things in her life that keeps her moving forward in life. It gives her hope that she will be rewarded for her suffering in heaven. She respects this man of GOD and entrusts her children to him. Would she trust I'm telling the truth if I told her, or would she hush me up as she usually does by saying, "Don't talk like that." For the good of everyone else, this will remain my secret. I do not want to betray the family or my pastor. I already know I'll somehow be at fault. Did I bring it on and provoke this man of God?

Age Sixteen; Where Are You, God?

This is hard to write about because this incident changed the trajectory of my life. It ravaged my trust in men, eroded my faith, and made me abandon religion. Because of my age, the wound carved a deep and painful gash in my heart. We had integrated Rev into our household since I was a small child. My parents trusted him, his wisdom and gentleness. My brothers and sister still speak highly of him and attribute where they are in life today because of his guidance and compassion. In recent years I have gone to family get-togethers and his name comes up in conversation. They speak of him as a saint. I have never shared this story of him to the family, because of their reverence for him, and I always wondered if they would believe me. I recognize that this story also happened for a reason of forgiveness. For him giving me the experience of complete betrayal by another human in this lifetime. My soul's request, to feel the total abandonment of a father, a spiritual father and a mortal one. For giving me the gift of feeling an all-encompassing separation from the whole with such a deep, excruciating understanding.

The struggle with these extraordinary betrayals is finding your way back from that separation. The only way back to the connection to one (God, the universe, the understanding of love) is through forgiveness. Being able to feel the extreme pain, release it, and then understand how it changed you through forgiveness is the experience. I now know that we are not our worst moments or actions. Yes, we don't know what we are capable of until an extreme circumstance or state of mind arises and we react or act upon it. And still it does not define us entirely. I would never have had the trust in a higher power to make it through some of my experiences without my deep faith, which also came from this same man. All my stories could not have been planned more perfectly than how they occurred. The magnificence of the universe in creating each one has bought me to the shared oneness with impeccable mastery. I am grateful for the life I have created around myself and for all of my stories. The magnificence of each story as they happened could not have been planned by an earthly presence. Thank-you.

My Childhood: Getting Over it

Have you wondered why people and experiences showed up in your life? Have you forgiven yourself first and accepted that you too are a soul having a human experience and you too have made bad decisions, and mistakes? Only then can you ask who needs forgiveness in your past so you can release and live your soul to its fullest?

Age Sixteen;
Change in Dad's Pocket

Reaching in . . . slowly

Trying not to wake my dad

Stealing change . . . for lunch

My Childhood: Getting Over it

High school lunch reminds me daily that I am poor. I avoid the lunch room and my friends because I cannot predict with any reliability that I will have the funds every day to buy a meal. I wait in the restrooms or the halls to empty before lunchtime so that my girlfriends don't see me to invite me. There are days when I secure cash for my go to meal, a bag of Muncho potato chips and an ice cream sandwich. The closest place to make the purchase with enough time to return is a few blocks away, a corner bodega. I eat alone and hang outside the back entrance of the school and wait for the bell to ring and the security guard to open the door. When I do not have the funds to buy a lunch, I wander across the street to the Sears and Roebuck ladies' room. I pick through the tall cigarette butt cans to find the longest used cigarettes and then relax, have a smoke in the lady's bathroom lounge, pretending to be an adult.

Dad regularly has coinage in his suit coat pocket, which hangs on the back of the dining room chair. He doesn't drive a car, so he makes sure he collects coins daily for bus fare. Every morning on my way out the door, I reach into his pocket quietly and I grab a handful of change. I justify the stealing; it is his responsibility to provide for me, isn't it?

If he is low on coinage, I leave at least enough to get himself downtown. I wonder if my siblings do the same each day? Hmmm . . . Is that why he consistently stocks his suit coat with so much more change than needed for bus fare?

On occasions when Dad isn't home in the a.m. and days his pockets are empty, a slight panic rises in me. What am I going to eat? Do I have hidden stashed coins? Should I hit my penny jar for a dollar? I must roll them; it is too embarrassing to pay with loose pennies. I know I can't go to Mom. Is there any fruit in the frig? My vigilance in earning cash is always on alert.

Age Sixteen; Change in Dad's Pocket

A mere $5 is a tremendous impact on my teenager's weekly routine and guarantee of eating during the day at school.

When I come into money by shoveling snow or raking leaves, I indulge myself at Sears. I buy chocolate by the quarter pound at the candy counter, and then I pamper myself with a cigarette. The negligible security I go through during those times gives me the belief that, ultimately, I'll have the capital to wield this same purchase power any way I wish. Again, this confidence is a mystery to me, yet I trust in that someday.

Children: you never know what kind of struggle they are going through. They appear to be okay and that everything at home is okay. Other times they act so outrageous we dismiss it as adolescent rebellion or a phase. I don't think anyone questioned my appearance at school, my behavior; and/or I blended in very well. Shame kept me from ever exposing myself, or asking for help. I had nothing to be ashamed of, I was surviving the best ways I knew. My situation was not of my conscious choosing or doing

I have become aware of teens and their needs. Why they don't participate in activities, because they don't have the money but are ashamed to verbalize it. Aware when my son's friends, held back when we went for lunch and making light of paying for it announcing it's my treat today. Letting them blend in and enjoy without feeling the shame. It's a great habit, this observation of others, especially children.

Age Sixteen; My First Sexual Experience

Sex

I read about it

Heard about it

Fantasized about it

Anticipated it

Made out and loved it

And then it happened

Trapped

Scraped

bleeding

one option . . . concede

He asks obliviously, "Was it good for you?"

unaware

My Childhood: Getting Over it

I am sixteen and have been dating for several months. He is twenty. We have made out extensively and have avoided having sex. Our plan for Saturday is that he will pick me and my brothers and sisters up at the corner and take them to Olympic Park. There he will give them money to play pinball games down the street at the arcade. We will then go to a park.

Today I am not prepared to have sex but expect to make out. His car has bucket seats in the front and rear which is always helpful in fighting off the act of sex. The ground outside is wet, and he finds a cement pad in front of a locked pavilion. The grass has grown around the cement pad to at least three feet high. As we make out, he acts more forceful than usual, and once he unbuckles my pants, he pulls them right off me. My backside lies on top of the concrete pad and I try to wiggle away, saying, "Stop." I feel the exposed knuckles on my backbone scrape against the hard, rough surface, taking skin with it. The more I attempt to shimmy up and away, the more agonizing my back becomes. Aggressive kisses muffle my pleads to stop, and the weight of his body 180 pounds on my 90-pound frame stops the squirming. I accept; today is the day I am losing my virginity.

It does not take long. The act itself is not painful because my back is excruciating and feels like it's bleeding. This supersedes any other pain at the moment.

After we dress and walk toward the car, he hugs me and asks, "Was it good for you?" Did he think my moaning was because of his thrusts, which were literally moving my body up and across the concrete slab?

I recognize how forceful he was and understand that he did not consider my feelings during his desire and intention to get inside me.

Age Sixteen; My First Sexual Experience

My words, actions, and body were never noticed or honored. I feel used and degraded. Not the storybook ending I have read about. His comment stays with me for days, and I question myself on how he dared ask me that. The struggle was not pleasurable, romantic, flirtatious, or fulfilling. As the knuckles on my vertebrae scab up and start to heal, they leave behind a reminder of that day. It is hard not to move my tailbone and not feel the scabs ripping open and the pain lingers. I didn't know what to expect in my future regarding sex with him. How disappointing the irrevocable act was after all the intrigue leading up to it.

This first intimate experience left me so disappointed. There was no comparison to the foreplay I had experienced and none of the pleasurable sensations accompanied this event. I have heard and read about others' sexual encounters, and they always amaze me. How can one individual's focus on his objective be so anesthetizing that he becomes unaware of the other's reaction, response, and, sometimes even existence? Ha, ha! I have to laugh. Was he aware of my presence, not my pussy, but me lying there in pain?

A callow man's testosterone drive can be uncontrollable. I can't pretend to understand men's tenacity about sex. I can only describe how it feels on the recipient's end. Can you see me, feel me? I'm here, receiving all this aggression and urgency. Do you not see it in my face and feel it in my body? It's as if I am watching you fuck me and I'm not here. I have to ask, who are you? You seemed like a nice enough guy, who showed me consideration and kindness, and now I know a different you. You showed me a vast contrast to who I thought you were.

It has helped to write about this experience. The writing brings out the words to describe the feelings coursing through me during the episode.

My Childhood: Getting Over it

Expressing the words and what my senses were struggling with releases some trauma my body has been holding in.

Finding an outlet to express trauma is so crucial to healing. Just sharing stories with a trusted friend releases pain. Find one story you can share to begin to feel and release. If you can't share, write about it, all of it, feelings, smells, and pain.

Age Sixteen; Miscarriage

Losing a life without knowing

No tears spent on grieving

Experiencing the pain

Feeling the release

Getting on with the day

Moving, climbing stairs, moving

Finally sleeping, resting

And moving again

Healing the body without knowing

My Childhood: Getting Over it

The pain starts just after midnight and comes in waves of cramps. At first, I think of bowel cramps, but the pain worsens, and my entire lower body is seizing as if held in a vice. The pain continues for hours, and I try to keep my sobs and moans low so my sister in the other bed across the room won't hear me. Early in the morning, I have a powerful urge to go to the bathroom and push. Never turning the lights on in the bathroom, I push several times and something forces its way out of me and plops into the toilet. Relief and exhaustion flood over me, and I walk back upstairs to my bedroom and fall asleep. My alarm goes off at six a.m. only an hour after I fall asleep, and I can barely get out of bed from exhaustion. I notice my sheets are bloody. I remove them and take them downstairs from the third floor to the basement and put them in the wringer washer to soak. I then get ready for school. I hear one of my brothers loudly commenting that there's something gross in the toilet. My mother shushes him and goes into the bathroom with a bucket and empties the toilet contents into the bucket, which she then takes out to the trash can behind the garage. I take a shower, get dressed, and catch the bus to school.

In between classes I go to the girls' room and when I wipe myself, I notice gooey, stringy, bloody mucus substances coming out of me. I do not understand what is happening to my body. I think I am having the worst period ever. After lunch and a class on the third floor, I just have to lie down. I go to the nurse's office and tell her I'm not feeling well and have to rest. She doesn't question me; I must look terrible. The next thing I know she is waking me up so I can get on the bus to go home.

I have been having sex for months. After the first experience, and having nothing to compare it to, experimenting begins in different positions, places. Sex starts to become enjoyable. I discover the plea-

Age Sixteen; Miscarriage

sures my body can give and finally experience my first orgasm, realizing Wow! That's what it's all about, that's the goal! I still do not realize that I had a miscarriage. I don't have a doctor, and Mom always takes care of us when we are ill. A few months later, I see a doctor when I become pregnant again and explain what happened with my period a while back. He tells me I miscarried. I could have become infected if any part of the placenta was still in me, and that I was a lucky lady. The physician told me that the amount of walking I did after the miscarriage kept the uterus discharging, keeping me safe. It mystifies him that I didn't seek treatment, and that I didn't understand that I had a miscarriage. He stresses that if this should happen again, I should immediately contact him to make sure I don't get an infection.

My mother, who gave birth to eleven children, never mentions a word to me about what she found in the toilet. She never approaches me to ask questions. I don't know if it connects to my period, a symptom of having sex, and I don't have anyone to discuss or share my questions with. At first, I assume that this pain and discharge would be a regular bodily function of releasing my boyfriend's ejaculate that stayed inside me. I do not understand how my period stopping correlates with being pregnant. Did I miss those classes in health education? I continue along with my regular routine as if it is now a new part of my life, which I would have to deal with whenever it happened. When the doctor explains it to me, I can't remember how many periods I had missed to figure out how far along in my pregnancy I was when I miscarried.

This was another incident in my life that I just pushed through. At sixteen, I had developed a pattern of "just keep moving forward." My mantra: "Do what

My Childhood: Getting Over it

you have to, to get through the day," and "This too shall pass." I had reached a point in my life where I considered nothing abnormal. I went through a remarkable amount of pain that night and didn't mention it to anyone. Once I felt relief, I continued through the day, experiencing exhaustion and bodily pain, still pushing on. Was I ever going to say enough or cry for help? Who was the person I could confide in? I worried about sounding and looking stupid. If I said enough, how would it help me, believing that there wasn't anything more or better for me? Asking for help was impossible for me and would be showing weakness. My heart aches recalling this story for the child who couldn't speak and just kept going. I wasn't confused about what was happening, I just had no clue.

The surrounding adults in my life were oblivious to my pregnancy, bloody sheets, fetus left in the toilet, and my exhaustion. My body took care of itself exactly how it should. I have since learned to listen to what my body is telling me through pain. I no longer ignore its warnings and act when I need to. It warns me in advance to pay attention to my partner, and my body.

Learning to listen to your body is one of the greatest gifts you can give yourself. Heeding its warnings will save you from suffering. Many times, we wait and wait to take care of ourselves and illnesses or call the doctor, hoping the pain, lump, soreness will go away, or not wanting to face the disease or diagnosis that we already know is working its way through our body. Attend to yourself and give yourself the love you deserve.

Age Eighteen;
An Adult

Forty-one days now

Separated from childhood

A child with a child

My Childhood: Getting Over it

Forty-one days have passed since my eighteenth birthday, and you are here. I sit on the steps of my mother's house, away from the hospital rules, prying visitors, and all-knowing interrupting nurses. I caress your damp hair as I lift off your yellow knitted cap. It's unseasonably warm today, in the 80s. I have you swaddled in three blankets, wearing your going-home outfit with its matching hat, sweater, and booties.

I gaze at your morsel of a soul, overwhelmed by the energy and depth of my love. Love this strong has never taken over my heart, and I tremble in awe of it.

Everything around me goes quiet. I am in the present moment with you, yes, the whole little package of you as I gently unravel your arms and legs and contemplate you. You are finally here, a miniature human, gazing back at me. I learn I am only a shadow in your eyes, and it doesn't matter; I connect with you, really unite in spirit with you, and grapple with an urgency rising in me. You are here, not a doll, or someone else's kid I am babysitting. Separate, no longer a part of me. You are out here in the world that I have learned not to trust, the world filled with danger, deceit, suffering, evil, and a place of injury.

I take in the measure of you, a six-pound, tiny individual giving yourself to my possession. To teach you what I know, to keep you safe, guide you, nurture you, and give you the confidence to stand in yourself with strength, compassion, and mostly to appreciate how significant you are.

Age Eighteen; An Adult

My love expands to envelop you. Our souls were physically connected and now we are spiritually and emotionally intertwined.

Can you feel it?

I try to hold on to the last fragments of my childhood as they slip aside and I prepare to embrace my way into adulthood. Authentic obligation, tiptoeing into who I am and how I will be with you, my first child.

My age and new responsibility represented adulthood to me. I began my journey into parenthood with the examples of my parents. I definitely knew what I did not want to repeat or use in my parenting role. Little did I know how little I knew. The love I was feeling was overwhelming and would be the powerful drive that would be my gauge in parenting. My history and patterns, my beliefs also impacted my relationship with this little boy I was entrusted with. My unconscious and even conscious beliefs enmeshed, integrated, and grew on him, and would now shape and develop patterns in his life.

I vividly remember an incident with my son when he was just a toddler. I was trying to keep him quiet during the hour-long service in church. The pastor's wife had instructed me to keep taking him to the restroom when he acted up and hit him with my hair brush. Her wisdom was that eventually he would learn to be quiet. The first time I did that and hit my son repeatedly with my brush, I saw horror, anger, and confusion on his face. I didn't think one so young could express such anger. I immediately stopped and apologized and hugged him. I couldn't bring myself to hit him ever again. That incident gave me a great lesson in watching his facial expressions and reactions.

My Childhood: Getting Over it

I try to use these gauges in the future to guide me. In seeing his reactions to mine. Teaching – learning, always growing, into who we are.... Changing.

I would encourage all my readers to observe all those around you and to allow them to impart knowledge through sheer observation.

What, patterns did you bring into your adult life, your relationships, and your decisions, your baggage. It's easy to think of our beliefs, and answers are the right ones, right? And each of us carries with us our unconscious and also conscious beliefs and actions, until they become awarenesses and we can look at them and our relationships with our eyes wide open.

EPILOGUE

I felt the tremendous responsibility I now held in my hands and also felt as if I had already lived a lifetime. I was ready to leave my father's reign of terror and fear and was anticipating a life of peace, one I wanted to create. Dreaming of having five boys and a house with a white picket fence. ` At eighteen, I did not know how much I was carrying into my adulthood and the profound impact this baggage of beliefs and patterns would have on my relationships, and life ahead. It took many years of searching, learning, recognizing, integrating, and transforming for me to be able to let go of this childhood. It is now a collection of stories, with an understanding of why they happened and how they impacted me. However, they no longer define me. What a blessing to be able to write them down and leave them. My hope is that anyone that reads this collection of stories can also know that their own stories are just that, stories. You have the power to take control of your present life, patterns, and identity. You can Get Over it! You can heal! You can let it go and live your authentic self without being haunted by your past, whatever it may have held.

My journey into adulthood and motherhood continued, with my children being one of my biggest teachers in life. Their honesty, trust, compassion, and understanding resonated with my inner child. Even at times when I didn't want to admit that their words or attitudes were their own expressions of themselves in the right form, energy, and delivery. My first child would scream out: Listen! See what it is they are telling you! Now as a grandmother, I can totally appreciate a child's expression of anger, joy, frustration, and more.

Not to admonish, control, or even change, but to allow it to come forth, in the form it presents itself in. Talking about it, how it feels, and what they want to do with those feelings. It has been a beautiful cycle, and I will continue to work on this rhythm with all the love I can give to it.

www.ingramcontent.com/pod-product-compliance
Lightning Source LLC
Chambersburg PA
CBHW072153100526
44589CB00015B/2214